Atlas of World History

The Early Modern World
1492–1783

BROWN
BEAR
BOOKS

Published by Brown Bear Books Limited

An imprint of:
The Brown Reference Group Ltd
68 Topstone Road
Redding
Connecticut 06896
USA
www.brownreference.com

ISBN: 978-1-933834-68-9

Editorial Director: Lindsey Lowe
Senior Managing Editor: Tim Cooke
Managing Editor: Rachel Tisdale
Editor: Helen Dwyer
Designer: Barry Dwyer

Library of Congress Cataloging-in-Publication Data available upon request

Picture Credits

Cover Image
Jupiter: photos.com

Artwork © The Brown Reference Group Ltd

The Brown Reference Group Ltd has made every effort to trace copyright holders of the pictures used in this book. Anyone having claims to ownership not identified above is invited to contact The Brown Reference Group Ltd.

Printed in the United States of America

Contents

Introduction

Atlas of World History **forms part of the Curriculum Connections series. The six volumes of this set cover all the major periods of the World History curriculum: The First Civilizations (4,000,000–500 BCE); The Classical World (500 BCE–600 CE); The Middle Ages (600–1492); The Early Modern World (1492–1783); Industrialization and Empire (1783–1914); and World Wars and Globalization (1914–2010).**

About this set

Each volume in *Atlas of World History* features thematic world and regional maps. All of the regional maps are followed by an in-depth article.

The volume opens with a series of maps that provide an overview of the world at particular dates. They show at-a-glance how the shape of the world changed during the period covered in the book. The rest of the volume is divided into regional sections, each of which covers a continent or part of a continent. Within each section, maps appear in broadly chronological order. Each map highlights a particular period or topic, which the accompanying article explains in a concise but accurate summary.

Within each article, two key aids to learning are located in sidebars in the margins of each page:

Curriculum Context sidebars indicate that a subject has particular relevance to certain key state and national World and American history guidelines and curricula. They highlight essential information or suggest useful ways for students to consider a subject or to include it in their studies.

Glossary sidebars define key words within the text.

At the end of the book, a summary Glossary lists the key terms defined in the volume. There is also a list of further print and Web-based resources and a full volume index.

About this book

The Early Modern World is a fascinating guide to the history of humankind from the time of Christopher Columbus to the American Revolutionary War.

The volume begins with a series of maps that present an overview of the grand themes of history at key dates between 1492 and 1783. The maps chart the shifting pattern of human settlement and the rise and fall of empires and states, in addition to reviewing the spread of trade and exploration on a world scale.

The regional maps that follow look more closely at the great events of the period: the Reformation and Enlightenment in Europe, the rise and fall of the dazzling Ottoman, Mughal, and Safavid empires, the European impact on the Americas, and the turmoil of Ming and Manchu China. There is also coverage of less familiar histories, such as those of the African Songhai empire and the Vietnamese state of Annam.

TYPOGRAPHICAL CONVENTIONS

World maps

FRANCE	state or empire
Belgian Congo	dependency or territory
Mongols	tribe, chiefdom or people
Anasazi culture	cultural group

Regional maps

HUNGARY	state or empire
Bohemia	dependency or territory
Slavs	tribe, chiefdom or people
ANATOLIA	geographical region
⚔	battle
•	site or town

The World in 1530

The expansion of the Ottoman empire took it into central Europe and North Africa; it dominated the Black Sea region. In South Asia, the Mughals had expanded south from Afghanistan into northern India. Meanwhile, the Portuguese and Spanish mariners were establishing trade networks and overthrowing empires, including the Aztec empire in the Americas.

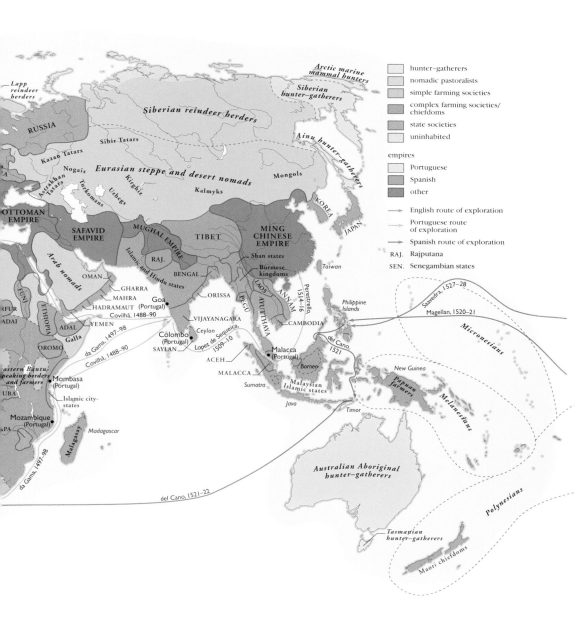

Lapp
reindeer
herders

RUSSIA

Kazan Tatars

Astrakhan
Tatars

Nogais

Turkomans

OTTOMAN
EMPIRE

SAFAVID
EMPIRE

Arab nomads

OMAN

GHARRA

MAHRA

HADRAMAUT

YEMEN

FUN

DFUR

ADAI

ADAL

Galla

OROMO

ETHIOPIA

UBA

astern Bantu-
peaking herders
and farmers

PA

Mombasa
(Portugal)

Islamic city-
states

Mozambique
(Portugal)

Malagasay

Madagascar

da Gama, 1497–98

Covilhã, 1488–90

da Gama, 1497–98

del Cano, 1521–22

Sibir Tatars

Eurasian steppe and desert nomads

Kirghiz

Uzbegs

MUGHAL EMPIRE

Islamic and Hindu states

RAJ.

BENGAL

ORISSA

VIJAYANAGARA

Ceylon

Colombo
(Portugal)

SAYLAN

Goa
(Portugal)

Covilhã, 1488–90

TIBET

Kalmyks

Mongols

Siberian reindeer herders

Arctic marine
mammal hunters

Siberian
hunter-gatherers

Ainu hunter-gatherers

MING
CHINESE
EMPIRE

Shan states

Burmese
kingdoms

PEGU

LAOS

AYUTTHAYA

ANNAM

CAMBODIA

ACEH

MALACCA

Sumatra

Malacca
(Portugal)

Lopez de Sequeira,
1509–10

Borneo

Malaysian
Islamic states

Java

Timor

KOREA

JAPAN

Taiwan

Perestrello,
1514–16

Philippine
Islands

del Cano,
1521

New Guinea

Papuan
farmers

Saavedra, 1527–28

Magellan, 1520–21

Micronesians

Melanesians

Polynesians

Australian Aboriginal
hunter-gatherers

Tasmanian
hunter-gatherers

Maori chiefdoms

- hunter-gatherers
- nomadic pastoralists
- simple farming societies
- complex farming societies/
  chiefdoms
- state societies
- uninhabited

empires

- Portuguese
- Spanish
- other

→ English route of exploration

→ Portuguese route
  of exploration

→ Spanish route of exploration

RAJ. Rajputana

SEN. Senegambian states

The World in 1600

Spain exploited its conquests in the Americas and reached the peak of its power. By 1600, it had seized Portugal. The Dutch were attempting to take over Portuguese trading bases worldwide. Russia had expanded to the Caspian Sea to the south and into Siberia to the west. The Mughals had created a Muslim empire in India, and in China, the Ming dynasty remained poweful despite facing many threats.

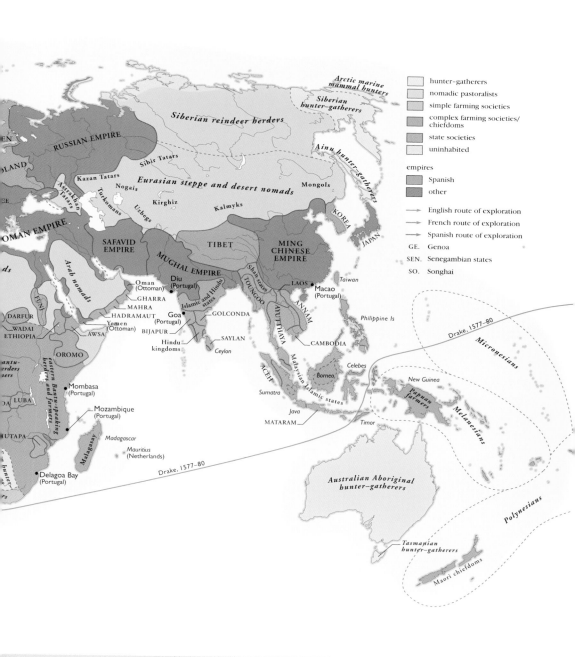

hunter-gatherers
nomadic pastoralists
simple farming societies
complex farming societies/ chiefdoms
state societies
uninhabited

empires
Spanish
other

→ English route of exploration
→ French route of exploration
→ Spanish route of exploration

GE. Genoa
SEN. Senegambian states
SO. Songhai

Arctic marine mammal hunters

Siberian hunter-gatherers

Siberian reindeer herders

Ainu hunter-gatherers

RUSSIAN EMPIRE

Sibir Tatars

Eurasian steppe and desert nomads

Mongols

Kazan Tatars

Astrakhan Tatars

Nogais

Turkomans

Uzbegs

Kirghiz

Kalmyks

KOREA

JAPAN

OMAN EMPIRE

SAFAVID EMPIRE

MUGHAL EMPIRE

TIBET

MING CHINESE EMPIRE

Arab nomads

Oman (Ottoman)

Diu (Portugal)

GHARRA

MAHRA

HADRAMAUT

Yemen (Ottoman)

AWSA

Islamic and Hindu states

TOUNGOO

Shan states

LAOS

Taiwan

Macao (Portugal)

DARFUR

WADAI

ETHIOPIA

OROMO

Goa (Portugal)

GOLCONDA

BIJAPUR

Hindu kingdoms

SAYLAN

Ceylon

AYUTTHAYA

ANNAM

CAMBODIA

Philippine Is

Drake, 1577–80

Micronesians

eastern herders and farmers

Bantu-speaking herders and farmers

LUBA

Mombasa (Portugal)

ACEH

Sumatra

Malaysian Islamic states

Borneo

Celebes

New Guinea

Papuan farmers

Melanesians

Mozambique (Portugal)

Java

MATARAM

Timor

MUTAPA

Madagascar

Malagasay

Mauritius (Netherlands)

Delagoa Bay (Portugal)

Drake, 1577–80

Australian Aboriginal hunter-gatherers

Tasmanian hunter-gatherers

Maori chiefdoms

Polynesians

The World in 1650

The Thirty Years' War had brought destruction and devastation to much of Europe. The power of Spain and the Holy Roman empire was broken, and France had emerged victorious over the Habsburgs. The Netherlands had taken control of much of the Portuguese trading empire, and the French and English had established colonies in North America. In Asia, the Manchus had swept away the Chinese Ming empire.

Greenland

Iceland (Denmark)

SCOTLAND

DENMARK

ENGLAND U.P.

FRANCE RE

PORTUGAL

SPAIN

G

Papal states

Algiers

MOROCCO

cam

St Louis (France)

TEKRUR

Portuguese Guinea

MALI

AKAN

Mossi states

Hausa states

SO

Elmina (Netherlands)

CONG

Lua (Port.

Arctic marine mammal hunters

sub-Arctic forest hunter-gatherers

plateau fishers and hunter-gatherers

west coast foraging, hunting and fishing peoples

desert hunter-gatherers

plains hunters

Iroquoian woodland farmers

Acadia

New France

Massachusetts Bay

New Amsterdam

Virginia

Pueblo farmers

plains farmers

Florida

Bahamas

Cuba

Belize

Jamaica

Hispaniola

Puerto Rico

VICE-ROYALTY OF NEW SPAIN

Essequibo

Surinam

Cayenne

Amazonian chiefdoms

Dutch Brazil
1642/54 to Portugal

Arawakan manioc farmers

VICE-ROYALTY OF PERU

Tupi-Guarani savanna and highland farmers

Portuguese Brazil

Hawaiian Islands

Polynesians

savanna hunter-gatherers

pampas hunter-gatherers

shellfish gatherers and marine mammal hunters

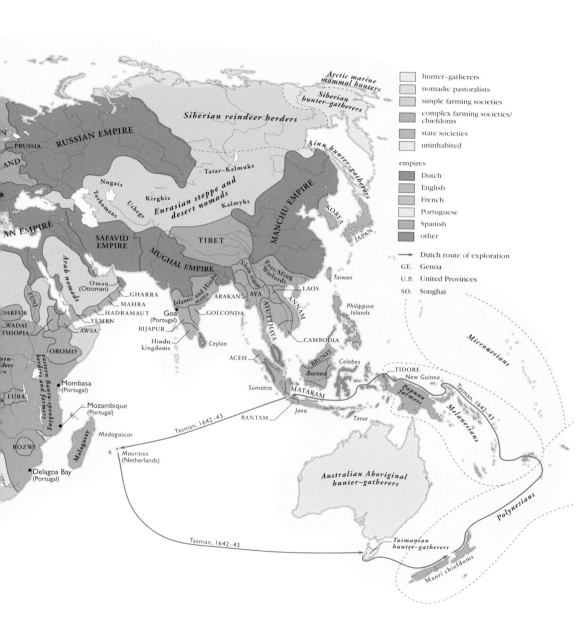

hunter-gatherers
nomadic pastoralists
simple farming societies
complex farming societies/chiefdoms
state societies
uninhabited

empires
Dutch
English
French
Portuguese
Spanish
other

→ Dutch route of exploration
GE. Genoa
U.P. United Provinces
SO. Songhai

Arctic marine mammal hunters

Siberian hunter-gatherers

Siberian reindeer herders

RUSSIAN EMPIRE

PRUSSIA

AND

Ainu hunter-gatherers

Nogais

Turkomans

Uzbegs

Kirghiz

Tatar–Kalmuks

Eurasian steppe and desert nomads

Kalmyks

MANCHU EMPIRE

KOREA

JAPAN

AN EMPIRE

SAFAVID EMPIRE

TIBET

Arab nomads

MUGHAL EMPIRE

Oman (Ottoman)

GHARRA

MAHRA

HADRAMAUT

YEMEN

AWSA

Islamic and Hindu states

Shan states

Post-Ming Warlords

LAOS

Taiwan

DARFUR

WADAI

THIOPIA

FUNJ

ARAKAN

AVA

ANNAM

Philippine Islands

Goa (Portugal)

GOLCONDA

BIJAPUR

Hindu kingdoms

Ceylon

AYUTTHAYA

CAMBODIA

ACEH

BRUNEI

Celebes

OROMO

eastern Bantu-speaking herders and farmers

LUBA

ders

Mombasa (Portugal)

Mozambique (Portugal)

Malagasy

Madagascar

ROZWI

Delagoa Bay (Portugal)

Bornea

Sumatra

MATARAM

BANTAM

Java

Timor

Micronesians

TIDORE

New Guinea

Papuan farmers

Melanesians

Tasman, 1642–43

Tasman, 1642–43

Mauritius (Netherlands)

Australian Aboriginal hunter-gatherers

Tasmanian hunter-gatherers

Polynesians

Maori chiefdoms

The World in 1715

Although France was now the greatest power in Europe, the Dutch dominated global trade. In northern Europe, Russia had replaced Sweden as the dominant force. In Asia, the Mughal empire in India was falling apart, while in China, the Manchus had expanded both north and south. Africa saw an Islamic revival in the north and the creation of an Omani Arab sultanate in Zanzibar. In North America, the English colonies had grown rapidly, and the English had taken control of French Canada.

Greenland

Arctic marine mammal hunters

sub-Arctic forest hunter-gatherers

plateau fishers and hunter-gatherers

west coast foraging, hunting and fishing peoples

desert hunter-gatherers

Pueblo farmers

plains hunters

Iroquoian woodland farmers

Rupert's Land

New France

Newfoundland

Nova Scotia

British American colonies

plains farmers

Louisiana

South Carolina

Florida

Cuba

Bahamas

Saint-Domingue

Belize

Hispaniola

Jamaica

VICE-ROYALTY OF NEW SPAIN

Mosquito Coast

Guyana

Cayenne

Hawaiian Islands

Polynesians

VICE-ROYALTY OF PERU

Arawakan manioc farmers

Tupi-Guarani savanna and highland farmers

VICE-ROYALTY OF BRAZIL

savanna hunter-gatherers

pampas hunter-gatherers

shellfish gatherers and marine mammal hunters

Iceland (Denmark)

DENMARK

GREAT BRITAIN

N

FRANCE

Ge

PORTUGAL

SPAIN

Papal states

MOROCCO

ALGIERS

Tunis

Tripc

cam

St Louis (France)

SEGU

TE.

KA

ARMA

SO

Hausa states

Portuguese Guinea

MALI

ASANTE

MO

OYO

Elmina (Netherlands)

CONG

Lua

(Portu

Cape C

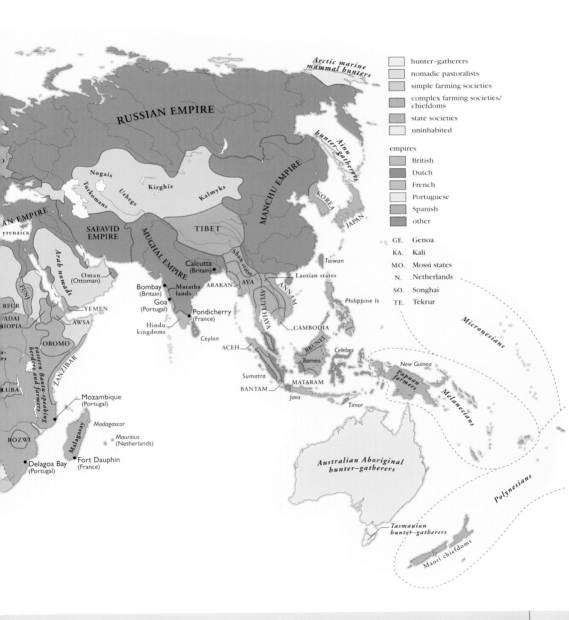

hunter-gatherers
nomadic pastoralists
simple farming societies
complex farming societies/
chiefdoms
state societies
uninhabited

empires

British
Dutch
French
Portuguese
Spanish
other

GE.   Genoa
KA.   Kali
MO.   Mossi states
N.   Netherlands
SO.   Songhai
TE.   Tekrur

Arctic marine mammal hunters

RUSSIAN EMPIRE

Ainu hunter-gatherers

Nogais

Turkomans

Uzbegs

Kirghiz

Kalmyks

MANCHU EMPIRE

KOREA

JAPAN

AN EMPIRE

yrenaica

SAFAVID EMPIRE

TIBET

MUGHAL EMPIRE

Arab nomads

Oman
(Ottoman)

FUN

RFUR

ADAI
IOPIA

YEMEN

AWSA

OROMO

ZANZIBAR

eastern Bantu-speaking borders and farmers

LUBA

Mozambique
(Portugal)

ROZWI

Delagoa Bay
(Portugal)

Bantu-speaking farmers

Madagasay

Fort Dauphin
(France)

Madagascar

Mauritius
(Netherlands)

Calcutta
(Britain)

Bombay
(Britain)

Goa
(Portugal)

Maratha lands

ARAKAN

AVA

Shan states

Pondicherry
(France)

Hindu kingdoms

Ceylon

Taiwan

Laotian states

ANNAM

AYUTTHAYA

CAMBODIA

ACEH

Sumatra

BANTAM

MATARAM

Java

Philippine Is

BRUNEI

Celebes

Borneo

Timor

New Guinea

Papuan farmers

Micronesians

Melanesians

Australian Aboriginal hunter-gatherers

Tasmanian hunter-gatherers

Polynesians

Maori chiefdoms

The World in 1783

Great Britain had won the long battle for dominance in the Americas and India, only to lose its American colonies in a bloody revolution. In Europe, Russia had destroyed Poland and pushed back the Ottoman frontier in the southwest, while Prussia had grown in power to rival Austria in central Europe. China was the world's greatest power, controlling much of central and Southeastern Asia, but in India, the British East India Company was dominant.

N

Greenland

Russian America

Arctic marine mammal hunters

sub-Arctic forest hunter–gatherers

plateau fishers and hunter–gatherers

west coast foraging, hunting and fishing peoples

Rupert's Land

Labrador

Iceland (Denmark)

DENMARK NOR

GREAT BRITAIN

N

Cook, 1768

FRANCE

Quebec

Newfoundland

Nova Scotia

PORTUGAL

SPAIN

FRANCE

Papal states

Vice-Royalty of New Spain

UNITED STATES OF AMERICA

MOROCCO

ALGIERS

Tunis

Tripo

Florida

camel

Hawaiian Islands

Bahamas

Saint-Domingue

Cuba

Jamaica

Belize

Hispaniola

Mosquito Coast

Vice-Royalty of New Granada

Guyana

Cayenne

St Louis (France)

FUTA TORO

AIR

KAARTA

SEGU

SO.

Hausa

states

KO

MO

Portuguese Guinea

FUTA JALON

ASANTE

DAHOMEY

BENIN

O

Polynesians

Marquesas Islands

Tuamotu Archipelago

Vice-Royalty of Peru

Vice-Royalty of Brazil

CONGO

Luar (Portu

Cook, 1770–71

Pitcairn Island

Vice-Royalty of Rio de la Plata

Cook, 1768

Cape Co

Cook, 1768–69

shellfish gatherers and marine mammal hunters

pampas hunter–gatherers

Falkland Islands (Spain)

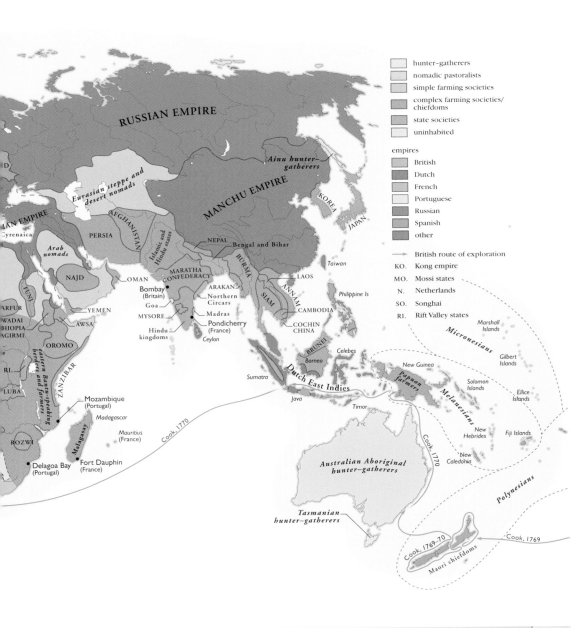

RUSSIAN EMPIRE

Ainu hunter–gatherers

MANCHU EMPIRE

Eurasian steppe and desert nomads

KOREA

JAPAN

AFGHANISTAN

PERSIA

Arab nomads

NEPAL

Bengal and Bihar

BURMA

Taiwan

NAJD

OMAN

MARATHA CONFEDERACY

Islamic and Hindu states

LAOS

ARAKAN

ANNAM

SIAM

Bombay (Britain)

Northern Circars

CAMBODIA

Philippine Is

Goa

MYSORE

Madras

Pondicherry (France)

COCHIN CHINA

Hindu kingdoms

Ceylon

Marshall Islands

Micronesians

BRUNEI

Celebes

Borneo

New Guinea

Gilbert Islands

Papuan farmers

Solomon Islands

Ellice Islands

Sumatra

Dutch East Indies

Melanesians

Mozambique (Portugal)

Java

Timor

New Hebrides

Fiji Islands

Madagascar

Mauritius (France)

Cook, 1770

New Caledonia

Malagasy

Cook, 1770

ROZWI

Delagoa Bay (Portugal)

Fort Dauphin (France)

Australian Aboriginal hunter–gatherers

Polynesians

Tasmanian hunter–gatherers

Cook, 1769

Cook, 1769–70

Maori chiefdoms

MAN EMPIRE

Cyrenaica

D

ARFUR

WADAI

HIOPIA

AGIRMI

FUN[...]

YEMEN

AWSA

OROMO

eastern Bantu-speaking herders and farmers

ZANZIBAR

RI.

LUBA

---

hunter-gatherers

nomadic pastoralists

simple farming societies

complex farming societies/ chiefdoms

state societies

uninhabited

empires

British

Dutch

French

Portuguese

Russian

Spanish

other

→ British route of exploration

KO. Kong empire

MO. Mossi states

N. Netherlands

SO. Songhai

RI. Rift Valley states

Reformation Europe

The first half of the 16th century in Europe was dominated by challenges to the authority of the Papacy and the Catholic Church.

ATLANTIC
OCEAN

Ireland
Irish Pale
Dublin

SCOTLA

Edinburgh
Flodden
1513

York

ENGLA

Norw

Wales

Oxford

Londo

1549,
Western
Rebellion

Bristol

Calais
1558 to
France

Rouen

Brittany
1491 to France

FRAN

Chambord

Loire

1527 to
France

La Rochelle

La Marc

1527 to
France

Bordeaux

1527 to
France

La Coruña

Santander

Pamplona

Navarre
1512 to Spain

Burgos

1521–22,
Comunero revolt

AN

Douro

SPAIN

Madrid

Aragon
1479 to Spain

Bar

PORTUGAL

Tagus

Castile
1479 to Spain

Lisbon

Valencia

Córdoba

Seville

Granada
Granada
1492 to Spain

Cartagena

BARBA

Tangier
Asilah

Ceuta

Melilla
1497 to Spain

Oran
1509 to Spain

Alg
151
154
emp

major faith, 1550

- Anglican
- Catholic
- Calvinist
- Lutheran
- Muslim
- Orthodox
- mixed

- state with significant Catholic minority, 1550
- state with significant Protestant minority, 1550
- borders, 1560
- territory controlled by Christian military orders, 1500
- Austrian Habsburg land
- Spanish Habsburg land
- Ottoman empire, 1492
- European territory lost to Ottomans by 1560
- Christian defeat by Ottomans
- major Ottoman siege
- Ottoman advance against Christian Europe
- popular uprising, with date
- major printing center, 15th–16th centuries
- Spanish *presidio* fort

Italian wars

- French victory
- Spanish Habsburg victory
- Venetian victory
- invasion route of Charles VIII of France, 1494

Christiania

SWEDEN
Stockholm

Vänern Vättern

Gotland

DENMARK–NORWAY

Copenhagen

Baltic Sea

Revel ESTONIA

LIVONIA

Riga

Pskov
1510 to Russia

Novgorod

Moscow

COURLAND

Western Dvina

Polotsk

RUSSIA

Smolensk

Königsberg

Danzig
ROYAL
PRUSSIA

PRUSSIA

Vilna

Minsk

Hamburg

Stettin

Brandenburg

Emden Bremen

Deventer

rdam

Utrecht Münster

HOLY
ROMAN
EMPIRE

Berlin

Lusatia

Leipzig
Wittenberg
Mühlberg
1547

Dresden

Prague

Vistula

Warsaw

Lithuania

Gomel

POLAND

Kiev

Cologne

Bonn

Saxony

Silesia

Krakow

Lemberg

Ukraine

etherlands

Luxembourg

Mainz

Frankfurt

Bamberg

Bohemia

Worms
1524–25,
Peasants War

Nuremberg

Moravia

1526 to Austrian
Habsburgs

MOLDAVIA
1504 Ottoman Vassal

Jedisan
1526 to Ottoman empire

Strasbourg

1482 to France

Augsburg

Ulm

Bavaria

1529
Vienna

Austria

Munich

Guns
1532

Buda

TRANSYLVANIA
1541 to
Ottoman empire

Jassy

Basel

Zürich

IMPERIAL HUNGARY

Gran

Franche
Comté

Swiss
Confederation

Berne
Geneva

Tyrol

Pieve di Cadore
1509

Trent
Venice

Mohács
1526

HUNGARY
1541 to Ottoman empire

Lyon

Savoy

Marignano
1515

Milan

rdois

Parma

Modena

VENICE

Belgrade

Danube

WALLACHIA

Bucharest

527 to
rance

Pavia
1525

Ravenna
1512

Black Sea

to France

Genoa

URBINO

Nish

Bulgaria

Provence

1481 to France

Piombino
Piombino

Florence
Siena

PAPAL STATES

Ragusa

Montenegro

Sofia

Orbetello

Corsica
to Genoa

Rome

Subiaco

NAPLES

Adrianople

Constantinople

Sardinia

Cagliari

Gargliano
1503

Naples

BENEVENTO

Cerignola
1503

Thessalonica

Rumelia

OTTOMAN

ANATOLIA

EMPIRE

Palermo

Messina

Reggio

SICILY

Sicily

Corfu
1537

Prevesa
1538

Athens

Morea

Izmir

Mediterranean
Sea

Monemvasia

1522
Rhodes

ST

gie
to Spain
to Ottoman empire

Tunis
1535 to Spain

MALTA
1551 1530 to Knights
of St John

Crete
to Venice

Candia

Reformation Europe

As the 15th century neared its close, the monarchies of western Europe consolidated their positions and brought civil wars within their territories to an end. Louis XI of France (r.1461–81) overcame his Burgundian rivals, Henry Tudor brought England's long Wars of the Roses to an end in 1485, and Ferdinand of Aragon and Isabella of Castile oversaw the unification of their kingdoms and the final conquest of Moorish Granada in 1492.

Fealty

The loyalty of a vassal or tenant to his lord.

As feudal relationships broke down, the near-independence of great nobles during the reigns of weak kings was gradually curtailed by the rise of administrators and financiers. Europe's monarchs became distributors of patronage in a world where finance was beginning to count for more than fealty.

Charles V and the Holy Roman empire

The old notion of a secular empire transcending the state endured. Charles VIII of France invaded Italy in 1494 in pursuit of such an aim, prompting a long struggle in which French, Spanish, and German armies rampaged through the peninsula. In 1519, Charles of Habsburg, grandson of both Ferdinand of Aragon and Maximilian I, became Emperor Charles V. The Holy Roman empire was weak and fragmented, but Charles now held the Austrian Habsburg lands in Spain, the Netherlands, Franche-Comté, and much of Italy, as well as Spain's new overseas possessions, creating a power bloc that dominated Europe until the late 17th century.

The defeat of Louis II of Hungary by the Ottomans at Mohács in 1526 raised the specter that the empire that would unify Europe might not even be a Christian one. In both central Europe and the Mediterranean, where Barbarossa's victory at Prevesa in 1538 ensured Ottoman and corsair (pirate) domination, Charles V took responsibility for halting the Ottoman advance.

Beginnings of the Reformation

Against this background of imperial commitments, the Reformation was played out. What began as a challenge by a monk, Martin Luther, to corrupt practices in the Church became an expression of German nationalism and then of local interests asserted against the emperor. The Peasants' Wars—uprisings partly fueled by religious unrest—were vigorously put down by the German nobility, who then began to adopt the reformed faith themselves, often for political reasons. Charles V won a crushing victory at Mühlberg over the Protestant nobles but otherwise did little to halt the spread of reform.

Curriculum Context

Studies of the Reformation usually begin with discontent among Europeans with the late medieval church, but also emphasize the importance of politics in its eventual success.

Challenges to the Papacy

The Papacy faced Luther's challenge hamstrung by a decline in the need for a unified Church (literacy, once the Church's preserve, had become more widely diffused in the previous two centuries) and by the widespread perception that the pope was merely a cynical participant in the complex web of Italian politics. The authority of the Church was challenged even by rulers with no particular religious motive: first by Ferdinand of Aragon, who threatened in 1508 to withdraw his kingdoms from obedience to the pope; in 1527 by Gustavus Vasa's seizure of Church lands in Sweden; and by Henry VIII of England, who repudiated papal authority in 1532.

Catholic compromise and response

The spread of printing gave the new demands for a more personal spirituality a mobility and resilience. Even as political compromise between the faiths was agreed in 1555 within the empire (the Peace of Augsburg) and between France and Spain in Italy in 1559 (the Treaty of Cateau-Cambrésis), the Catholic response was taking shape: the Council of Trent formulated a vigorous statement of Catholic doctrine, and the Jesuit Order was adopted as the spearhead of a new pastoral effort.

Curriculum Context

Explaining the aims and policies of the Catholic Counter-Reformation and assessing the impact of religious reforms and divisions on life in Europe are key to world history curricula in the 16th century.

Counter-Reformation Europe

In the second half of the
16th century, conflict
between Catholics and
Protestants continued and
Spain faced revolt in the
Netherlands.

O'Neill's rebellion,
1593–1603

O'Donnell's rebellion,
1594–1601

Irish Pale

Ireland • Dublin

Fitzmaurice's
rebellion,
1579

Kinsale
1601

Southamp
Plymouth

Spanish Armada, 1588

Je

La Ro

Be

Drake, Norris
1589

La Coruña
Santiago de
Compostela
Santander
Bilbao

Drake, Norris
1589
Vigo
Pamplona
Nav

Valladolid *Duero*

ATLANTIC
OCEAN

Salamanca
The Escorial
Madrid

Tagus
Alcántara
1580
Toledo

Valenc

Lisbon
Drake, Norris
1589

Córdoba

SPAIN

Cartagena

Seville
Morisco revolt,
1569–71

Howard, Essex
1596 Cádiz

to West Indies

Tangier • Ceuta

Mostagane

Melilla

Alcazarquivir
1578

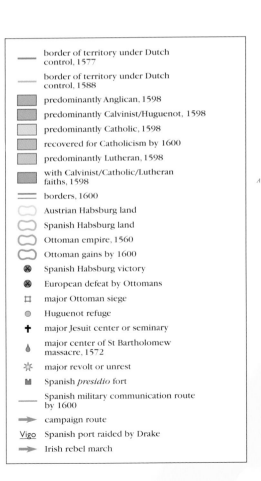

	border of territory under Dutch control, 1577
	border of territory under Dutch control, 1588
	predominantly Anglican, 1598
	predominantly Calvinist/Huguenot, 1598
	predominantly Catholic, 1598
	recovered for Catholicism by 1600
	predominantly Lutheran, 1598
	with Calvinist/Catholic/Lutheran faiths, 1598
	borders, 1600
	Austrian Habsburg land
	Spanish Habsburg land
	Ottoman empire, 1560
	Ottoman gains by 1600
⊗	Spanish Habsburg victory
⊗	European defeat by Ottomans
⊟	major Ottoman siege
○	Huguenot refuge
†	major Jesuit center or seminary
⬧	major center of St Bartholomew massacre, 1572
☼	major revolt or unrest
⋈	Spanish *presidio* fort
	Spanish military communication route by 1600
➜	campaign route
Vigo	Spanish port raided by Drake
➜	Irish rebel march

North
Sea

Baltic
Sea

rgh

TLAND

York

GLAND

Christiania

SWEDEN

Stockholm

Vänern Vättern

Copenhagen

Revel

Gotland

Courland
1561 to Poland

Riga

ESTONIA

Lake
Peipus

Livonia
1561 to Poland

DENMARK–NORWAY

Elbe

Netherlands
Amsterdam
Leiden

London
terbury
chelsea
Rye

Dunkirk
St Omer
Douai
1567–68
Rouen
Ivry
1590
Meaux
Dreux
1562
Orléans
Fléche
Fontaine-Française
1562
Bourges
Charolais
La Roche-L'Abeille
1569
Lyon

FRANCE

Toulouse

Perpignan

ANDORRA

ona

Antwerp
Breda
1586
Mons
Liège
Doullens
Reims
Verdun
Port-à-Mousson
Nancy
Troyes
Dôle
Franche-
Comté
Neuchâtel
Geneva

Savoy

Avignon

Aix

Balearic
Islands

Corsica
to Genoa

Sassari

Sardinia

Cagliari

Zutphen
1586
Maastricht
Hesse-
Kassel
Trier
Mainz
Lower
Palatinate
Strasbourg
Molsheim

Swiss
Confederation

HOLY
ROMAN
EMPIRE

Anhalt

Fulda
Nassau
Bamberg
Würzburg
Ansbach
Ingolstadt
Dillingen
Württemberg

Tyrol

Milan

Parma

GENOA

Genoa

Piombino
Porto Longone
Orbetello

Brandenburg

Saxony

Bohemia
Prague
Upper
Palatinate

Bavaria

Danube
Vienna

Austria

Graz
Neuhaus

Lusatia
Silesia
Glatz

Kuttenberg

Olmütz
Moravia
Brünn

IMPERIAL
HUNGARY

Trnava

Gran
Buda
Keresztes
1596

HUNGARY

Stettin

Königsberg

Danzig
Royal
Prussia

1569 to Poland

Warsaw

POLAND

PRUSSIA

Vistula

Krakow

TRANSYLVANIA

Po

Modena

PAPAL STATES

Venice

VENICE

Ravenna
URBINO

Tuscany

Siena

Rome

Corsica

Sardinia

SARDINIA

Cagliari

Belgrade

WALLACHIA

Bucharest

Danube

Nish

Bulgaria

Sofia

Black Sea

Ragusa

Montenegro

OTTOMAN

Adrianople

Constantinople

Thessalonica

Rumelia

ANATOLIA

EMPIRE

NAPLES

Naples

BENEVENTO

SICILY

Palermo

Sicily

Messina

Don John, 1572

Tunis

1569, 1574
1572

MALTA
1565

Don John, 1571

Mediterranean
Sea

Ottoman fleet, 1574

Lepanto
1571

Morea

Athens

Izmir

Monemvasia

Rhodes

Candia

Crete

1560

Counter-Reformation Europe

The peace agreements of the 1550s were greeted with relief in a Europe which, despite sustained economic growth since 1510, had known anything but peace. Yet the relief was short-lived. Religious conflict broke out in France and the Netherlands, while the Baltic lands of the former Teutonic Knights became a battleground for Polish, Danish, Swedish, and Russian armies.

At the same time, Europe's climate entered a two-century-long mini-ice age. Rivers froze in the long, cold winters, while the cool, wet summers all but wiped out the recent advances in agriculture.

Curriculum Context

Students are often asked to analyze the beliefs and ideas of the leading Protestant reformers, such as Martin Luther and John Calvin.

Huguenot
French Protestant.

Calvinism

The Reformation entered a new phase in the 1560s with the spread of Calvinism, more uncompromising and radical than Lutheranism. Scotland adopted the new faith in 1560, and its growth in the Netherlands underlay the Dutch revolt against Spanish rule in 1566. Above all, Calvinism unified and motivated the Huguenot minority in France. By 1600, almost 40 percent of Europe's population had renounced the Catholic faith. In Germany, the principle in the Peace of Augsburg that a prince was to determine the religion of his subjects allowed Protestantism to take root.

The Huguenots

In France, the Huguenots included many important figures in the royal administration and much of the nobility, including Henry of Navarre. The Huguenots took up arms in 1562 and remained a threat to the French crown, despite a string of military defeats and the slaughter of 30,000 men and women in the 1572 Massacre of Saint Bartholomew. Henry of Navarre renounced his faith to become Henry IV, first Bourbon king of France. He offered the Huguenots toleration, but the threat to the monarchy remained.

The Catholic Church

The Church's response to the Reformation was a pastoral and doctrinal offensive: the spread of colleges of the formidable Jesuit Order; the revival of the medieval Inquisition; the establishment of an Index of Prohibited Books; and a clearer restatement of the nature of Catholic faith than ever before. Politically, the Church found a champion in Philip II of Spain willing and able to take military action against its enemies.

Challenges to Spain

The challenges facing Philip II of Spain were many, and his administration was strained to the limit despite vast quantities of American silver that flowed through Spain. Faced with the Ottoman threat, he abandoned the effort to hold Tunis. Philip put down the revolt of the Moriscos (converted Moors) of southern Spain and acquired the crown of Portugal. He also struggled to meet the most serious threat to Habsburg authority, the Dutch revolt. On his behalf, the dukes of Alva and Parma recaptured most of the southern Netherlands. But from 1571, Dutch corsairs (the "Sea Beggars'") cut the Spanish sea route to the Netherlands, and in 1585, the hard-pressed Hollanders received military support from Protestant England.

England and Spain at war

England had seen the final triumph of Protestantism only in 1563, after Mary Tudor's brief and bloody reimposition of Catholicism (1553–58). Queen Elizabeth's position was secured in 1587 by the execution of her Catholic cousin and focus for discontent, Mary Queen of Scots. Philip II reacted to English support for the Dutch by sending the great naval expedition known as the Armada to spearhead a full-scale invasion in 1588. It failed, largely through violent weather and poor planning, but the threat of Spanish military intervention in England remained real until the end of the century.

Jesuit Order

The Society of Jesus, a Roman Catholic order founded by Saint Ignatius Loyola in 1534 to carry out missionary and educational work and attempt to halt the spread of Protestantism.

Sweden and the Baltic

In the two centuries between 1520 and 1720, Sweden extended its territory and dominated the Baltic region of northern Europe.

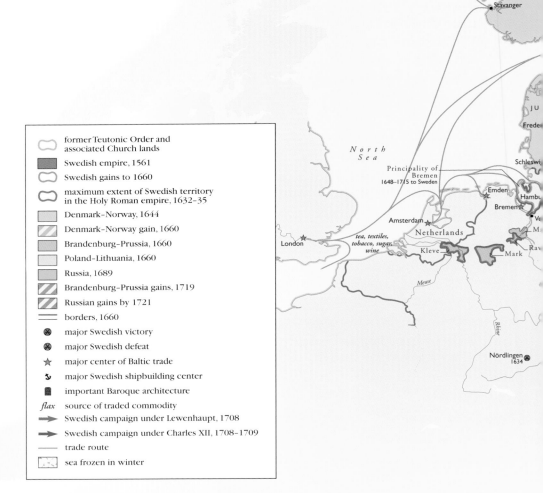

M

	former Teutonic Order and associated Church lands
	Swedish empire, 1561
	Swedish gains to 1660
	maximum extent of Swedish territory in the Holy Roman empire, 1632–35
	Denmark–Norway, 1644
	Denmark–Norway gain, 1660
	Brandenburg–Prussia, 1660
	Poland-Lithuania, 1660
	Russia, 1689
	Brandenburg–Prussia gains, 1719
	Russian gains by 1721
	borders, 1660
✪	major Swedish victory
✪	major Swedish defeat
★	major center of Baltic trade
⚓	major Swedish shipbuilding center
▮	important Baroque architecture
flax	source of traded commodity
➡	Swedish campaign under Lewenhaupt, 1708
➡	Swedish campaign under Charles XII, 1708–1709
—	trade route
░	sea frozen in winter

Bergen

Stavanger

North Sea

J U

Freder

Schleswi

Principality of Bremen 1648–1715 to Sweden

Emden

Hambu

Bremen

Amsterdam

Netherlands

tea, textiles, tobacco, sugar, wine

London

Kleve

Mark

Rav

Ve

M

Meuse

Rhine

Nördlingen 1634

LAPLAND

ARCHANGEL

Västerbotten
1560–1661 to Sweden

Luleå

1560–95
to Sweden

1658–1660 to Sweden
1660 to Denmark-Norway

Umeå

Trondheim
dheim

Jämtland
1645 to Sweden

Ångermanland

Gulf of Bothnia

Lake
Onega

Härjedalen

Medelpad

Österbotten

Vasa
Storkyra
1714

Finland

Karelia
1617 to Sweden
1721 to Russia

Dalecarlia

Falun

Gävle

Nystad

timber

Nyland

Vyborg

Lake
Ladoga

Christiania

*copper, iron,
timber*

Åland Is

Åbo

Helsingfors
(Helsinki)

St Petersburg

Stolbovo

Uppsala

Uppland

SWEDEN

Västerås

Stockholm

1720

Estonia
1561 to Sweden
1721 to Russia

Narva

1700

RUSSIA

Drottningholm

1714

Dagö
1582 to Sweden
1721 to Russia

Revel

1610 to Sweden
1617 to Russia

Ingria
1583, 1617 to Sweden
1595, 1721 to Russia

Södermanland

1718

Jerwen
1582 to Sweden
1721 to Russia

*flax, hemp,
hides*

Novgorod

Linköping

Vänern

Visby

Gotland
1645 to Sweden

Windau

Ösel
1645 to Sweden
1721 to Russia

Livonia
1582 to Sweden
1721 to Russia

Lake
Peipus

Tver

eborg

Westgotland

Vättern

Ostgotland

Pskov

Volga

Jönköping

Courland

Riga
Kircholm
1605

Moscow

Småland

Calmar

Öland

Libau

Mitau

Kokenhausen
1601

*flax, furs, grain,
hemp, timber*

singborg

1658
to Sweden

Blekinge

Brömsebro

Baltic Sea

Western Dvina

Polotsk

Klushino
1610

Skane
The Sound
1658

nagen
1658

1658 to Sweden
1660 to Denmark-
Norway

Ermeland
1629 to Sweden
1635 to Brandenburg-
Prussia

Memel

Samogitia

Vitebsk

Smolensk

Bornholm

Andrusovo

rania
weden

Kolberg

East Pomerania

Königsberg

Vilna

Holowczyn
1708

Mogilev

Vismar

Stralsund

Danzig

Elbing

*flax, grain,
hemp, timber*

Minsk

Lesnaya
1708

Starodub

klenberg

Stettin

Stuhm
1629

Prussia
Polish suzerainty until
1657/60

Grodno

Gomel

Gorki

randenburg

Fehrbellin
1675

Berlin

Poznan

Pultusk
1656

Vistula

Warsaw

Bug

Pinsk

Pripet

POLAND

Podolesia

Kiev

Ukraine

eld
1631

Saxony
Dresden

grain
1656

Lublin

Desna

OMAN
RE

Jankau
1645

Breslau

Oder

Volhynia

Poltava
1709

Prague

Klissow
1702

Krakow

Lemberg
(Lvov)

Zaporogian
Cossacks

Dnieper

Ochakov

Sweden and the Baltic

Late-medieval trade in the Baltic region was dominated by the Hanseatic League; its politics by the Hanseatic League and by the united kingdoms of Denmark–Norway and Sweden. The Hanseatic trading network, centered on Lübeck, stretched from London to Novgorod.

Naval stores
The raw materials needed for shipbuilding, such as timber, flax, hemp, pitch, and tar.

Control of the river ports that handled Baltic products—grain, copper, furs, and the naval stores that made possible Europe's overseas expansion—was central to the region's politics.

Swedish expansion

In the early 16th century, the hold of the Teutonic Knights on the eastern Baltic began to weaken, and English and Dutch merchants began to rival those of the Hanseatic League. In 1520, the Swedes under Gustavus Vasa rebelled against Christian II of Denmark and were supported by Lübeck. The victorious Swedes then joined a concerted effort by Lübeck's rivals to break the Hanseatic hold on Baltic trade. Swedish expansion was made possible by an efficient royal administration and a strictly enforced system of military service.

Control of Baltic trade

An early spur to Swedish expansion was the English establishment of a trade route to Russia via Archangel, bypassing the Baltic altogether. Thereafter, Swedish territorial gains were aimed at control of the Baltic river ports, through which grain and naval stores flowed to western Europe and beyond. The conquest of Livonia brought customs revenues equal to 25 percent of Swedish state income. Throughout the period, the Dutch hold on Baltic trade increased steadily, sometimes in partnership with Sweden, sometimes in opposition. The advanced Swedish metallurgical industry around Falun was entirely financed from Amsterdam, but a Dutch fleet helped destroy Swedish naval power off Öland in 1676.

Sweden against Russia and Poland

The Livonian War (1557–82) against Russia gained Sweden the whole of Estonia. Polish–Swedish rivalry became open warfare after the deposition in 1598 of Sigismund III, Vasa ruler of both kingdoms, from the Swedish throne. The Swedes acquired Karelia from the hard-pressed Russian czar (ruler) in return for aid and then extended their hold into eastern Karelia and Ingria by the Treaty of Stolbovo (1617).

The Thirty Years' War

Under Gustavus Adolphus (r.1611–32), a campaign against Poland secured Livonia and ensured that, when Gustavus intervened in the Thirty Years' War in 1630, the Swedish army was formidably experienced as well as tactically superior to the imperialist forces it faced. A crisis came when Gustavus was killed at Lützen (1632) and his army defeated at Nördlingen (1634), but Swedish fortunes were restored by Axel Oxenstierna and Lennart Torstensson, engineer of the crushing victory over the imperial forces at Jankau (1645) and a punitive invasion of Denmark in 1643–44. Swedish gains by 1648 included West Pomerania, the ports of Stettin and Wismar, and the former dioceses of Bremen and Verden.

Diocese
The territory under the authority of a bishop.

The Great Northern War

The last phase of Swedish greatness came under Charles XII (r.1697–1718), whose reign was devoted largely to the Great Northern War against an alliance of Russia, Denmark, and Poland. Charles soon defeated the Danes and in 1700, destroyed a Russian army five times the size of his own at Narva. Victories against Poland and Saxony followed and in 1708, Charles marched east. Russian scorched-earth tactics drew him south to pursue an alliance with Ukrainian Cossacks. At Poltava in 1709, the exhausted Swedes were routed by a Russian army. By 1721, all Swedish possessions southeast of the Baltic were in Russian hands.

Scorched-earth tactics
The deliberate destruction of property and resources, so that an invading army cannot use them.

The Thirty Years' War

The causes of the Thirty Years' War that raged across Europe from 1618 to 1648 were partly religious and partly political.

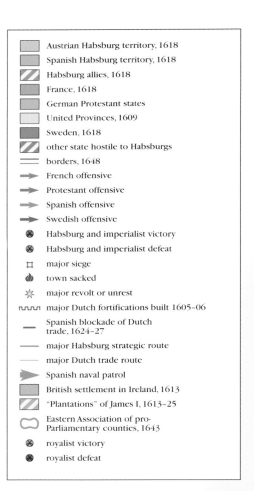

Austrian Habsburg territory, 1618

Spanish Habsburg territory, 1618

Habsburg allies, 1618

France, 1618

German Protestant states

United Provinces, 1609

Sweden, 1618

other state hostile to Habsburgs

borders, 1648

French offensive

Protestant offensive

Spanish offensive

Swedish offensive

Habsburg and imperialist victory

Habsburg and imperialist defeat

major siege

town sacked

major revolt or unrest

major Dutch fortifications built 1605–06

Spanish blockade of Dutch trade, 1624–27

major Habsburg strategic route

major Dutch trade route

Spanish naval patrol

British settlement in Ireland, 1613

"Plantations" of James I, 1613–25

Eastern Association of pro-Parliamentary counties, 1643

royalist victory

royalist defeat

Auldearn
1645

to Greenland,
Newfoundland and
Shetlands fisheries

ippermuir
644

North
Sea

SWEDEN

Stockholm

Vänern

Vättern

Baltic Sea

Edinburgh

Bishops' Wars,
1639–40

5

Newburn
1640

England

ton Moor
644

York

Preston
1648

Hull
1643

Nottingham

Naseby
1645

Fenland revolt,
1630–38

Oxford
1642–6

47

Putney Debates,
1647

London
1647

Downs
1639

Turnham
Green
1643

Dunkirk

Dunkirkers

Amsterdam

Breda

Antwerp

Brussels

Spanish
Netherlands
1642–46

FLANDERS

DENMARK–NORWAY

Christian IV, 1625

Mansfeld, 1626

Friedrichstadt

Bremen

Lübeck

Copenhagen

to Baltic
ports

Gustavus Adolphus, 1631–32

West
Pomerania

Stralsund
1628

Wismar
Mecklenberg

Kolberg

East Pomerania

Danzig
Royal
Prussia

Königsberg

PRUSSIA

Magdeburg
1631

Ravensberg

Westphalia

Brandenburg

Landsberg

Frankfurt

Wallenstein, 1627–28

Oder

Vistula

POLAND

UNITED
PROVINCES

Kleve

Mark

Hesse

HOLY
ROMAN EMPIRE

Frankfurt

Anhalt

Lutter
1626

Lützen
1632

Saxony

Breitenfeld
1651

Bayreuth

White Mountain
1620

Prague

Bohemia

Silesia

Krakow

'Nu-pieds',
1639–40

Paris

Spinola 1620

Heidelberg

Lower
Palatinate

ALSACE

Rhine

Ansbach

Nördlingen
1634

Regensburg

Moravia

Bethlen Gabor, 1619

George Rákóczy, 1645

Orléans

Loire

Bourges

1634

1634, 1637–48

Württemberg

Breisach

Ferla, 1633

Munich

Bavaria

Austria

Vienna

Danube

Styria

TRANSYLVANIA

Guyenne revolt,
641, 1645

Chatolais

FRANCE

Franche
Comté

SWISS
CONFEDERATION

1629

Tyrol

Salzburg

Carinthia

IMPERIAL HUNGARY

Gran

Buda

HUNGARY

guenots,
21–28

Peasant 'Croquants',
1636–37, 1643–45

Lyon

Geneva

SAVOY

1637–48

Turin

MILAN

Po

Milan

Mantua

Venice

Carniola

OTTOMAN
EMPIRE

deaux

Languedoc revolt,
1641, 1643–45

Genoa

PARMA

MODENA

Ravenna

VENICE

Toulouse

Avignon

GENOA

PAPAL STATES

Montenegro

Marseille

Provence revolt,
1639, 1643–45

1646

Florence

TUSCANY

Piombino

Porto Longone

PIOMBINO

Orbetello

Ragusa

Perpignan

1640–52

Roussillon
1642 to France

NDORRA

Catalan revolt,
1640

Barcelona

Corsica
to Genoa

Rome

NAPLES

1647

Naples

BENEVENTO

Palma

Balearic
Islands

Sardinia

SARDINIA

Cagliari

Palermo

1647

Messina

SICILY

Mediterranean
Sea

Sicily

MALTA

The Thirty Years' War

The "crisis of the 17th century" brought social upheaval, religious violence, and economic hardship across Europe from Portugal to Russia. Monarchs tried to increase their power at the expense of the nobility, local corporations, and the peripheral regions.

Curriculum Context

In some states, students are asked to analyze the causes of the Thirty Years' War and other religious conflicts of the 16th and 17th centuries.

Religious tensions abounded, heightened by the uncompromising stances of both Calvinism and Counter-Reformation Catholicism. In England and France, they gave an edge to political and social struggles. In the shifting alliances of the Thirty Years' War, religious affiliation was often little more than a badge for armies recruited from all faiths or for princes who changed religion to further a political advantage.

Richelieu and Mazarin

After the assassination of Henry IV in 1610, France underwent a period of weak government until Cardinal Richelieu became chief minister in 1624. The Huguenots demanded concessions and rose in revolt again. Richelieu laid siege to their chief stronghold, La Rochelle; the defenders were starved into submission. Thereafter Richelieu concentrated on dismembering the Habsburg empire. In the1640s, Richelieu and his successor Mazarin had military success in Flanders, the Rhineland, Italy, and the Pyrenees, and sponsored revolts in Portugal, Catalonia, Sicily, and Naples. Spain's empire appeared doomed.

Thirty years of war

The Thirty Years' War consisted of several stages. First, the Bohemian–Palatinate war (1618–23), in which a Bohemian Protestant and Transylvanian threat to Habsburg Vienna was defeated and the Calvinist Lower Palatinate was conquered by imperial and Spanish troops. Second, the Danish war (1625–29), in which an intervention on behalf of the German Protestants by Denmark was shattered at Lutter, and the Edict of

Edict

A proclamation of a law.

Restitution strengthened the position of the Catholics in Germany. Third, the Swedish war (1630–35), in which Sweden briefly carried the war to the heart of Catholic southern Germany. Fourth, the French–Swedish war (1635-48), in which the French defeated successive Spanish invasions and undertook counteroffensives against all the Spanish possessions, Sweden defeated the imperialists, and various armies spread unprecedented devastation over much of Germany before a peace was agreed.

Difficulties for Spain

Spain's role as Catholic champion of Europe was the greatest casualty of the war. The years of relative peace in the early 17th century were wasted, and the reform program initiated after 1621 by the chief minister Olivares could not be sustained, as the cost of financing a war effort across the continent escalated while silver revenues dwindled. With the revolts of Catalonia and Portugal in 1640, Spain was forced to divert resources to deal with domestic difficulties.

Civil war in Britain

James VI and I of Scotland and England planted Ulster with Protestant settlers. Constitutional and religious opposition to his son Charles I led to war in Scotland (1639–40), to a massacre of Ulster Protestants, and then to civil war in England. The victory of his Parliamentary enemies did not end unrest; the king was executed in 1649, and a Commonwealth established under Oliver Cromwell.

Dutch success

The Dutch alone gained from Europe's long, grim war. By weathering years of Spanish assaults, they preserved their trading empire, won their independence, and set about commercial expansion. By 1650, Amsterdam's financiers dominated the entire European economy.

Planted
Deliberately sent to colonize an area for political reasons.

Curriculum Context

An important aspect of the English civil war is its lasting effect on government, religion, economy, and society.

Europe and Louis XIV

Louis XIV of France spent his long reign (1643–1715) attempting to make France the dominant power in Europe.

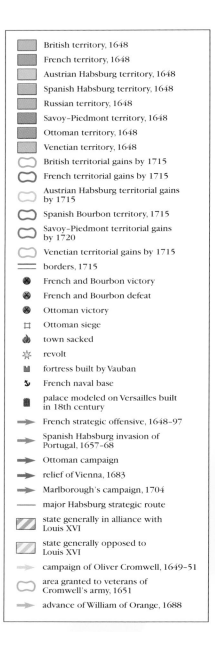

British territory, 1648
French territory, 1648
Austrian Habsburg territory, 1648
Spanish Habsburg territory, 1648
Russian territory, 1648
Savoy–Piedmont territory, 1648
Ottoman territory, 1648
Venetian territory, 1648
British territorial gains by 1715
French territorial gains by 1715
Austrian Habsburg territorial gains by 1715
Spanish Bourbon territory, 1715
Savoy–Piedmont territorial gains by 1720
Venetian territorial gains by 1715
borders, 1715
French and Bourbon victory
French and Bourbon defeat
Ottoman victory
Ottoman siege
town sacked
revolt
fortress built by Vauban
French naval base
palace modeled on Versailles built in 18th century
French strategic offensive, 1648–97
Spanish Habsburg invasion of Portugal, 1657–68
Ottoman campaign
relief of Vienna, 1683
Marlborough's campaign, 1704
major Habsburg strategic route
state generally in alliance with Louis XVI
state generally opposed to Louis XVI
campaign of Oliver Cromwell, 1649–51
area granted to veterans of Cromwell's army, 1651
advance of William of Orange, 1688

Europe and Louis XIV

The Thirty Years' War concluded the conflicts that had threatened Europe since the Reformation and brought a revulsion against religious and social extremism. Only in Britain, where Cromwell's regime faced mounting discontent until it collapsed in 1660, did the radical opponents of the existing social order achieve power.

Curriculum Context

Using France as an example of a strong bureaucratic monarchy, students can analyze the state's character, development, and sources of wealth.

There was a general extension of royal control over the affairs of the state, and the doctrine of the absolute power of the monarch emerged. In France, local administration was put in the hands of officials while aristocrats were required to dance attendance on the king at his court, and representative institutions were stripped of the power to criticize the government.

Changing alliances

From 1648, Louis XIV systematically pursued his ambition of supplanting Habsburg Spain as Europe's dominant power. The Netherlands allied itself with Spain against France and England. Under Cromwell and the later Stuart kings, England took a pro-France, anti-Spain stance, leading to a series of damaging naval wars with the Netherlands. The accession of the Dutchman William of Orange to the English throne in 1688–89 led in turn to Anglo–French enmity.

Rise of Austria, decline of Sweden

Austria emerged as a power, while Spanish strength waned. Sweden suffered a defeat at Fehrbellin while supporting Louis XIV against the Netherlands and thereafter shrank from direct involvement in western Europe. In Italy, Savoy eclipsed Habsburg Milan, while the Spanish possessions in the south survived the French-supported revolts of the 1640s but passed to Austrian control after 1713, as Spain's European territories were shared out between the new Bourbon king of Spain, Philip V, and the Austrian Habsburgs.

Louis XIV's successes and failures

Louis relied for most of his reign on a small group of highly competent ministers: Colbert (responsible for economic and financial policy, and building up the armed forces), Louvois (minister of war), Vauban (an engineer whose fortresses secured the northern and eastern frontiers), and a group of exceptional generals (Turenne, Condé, Luxembourg, and Villars). France fought four major wars in his reign, making substantial territorial gains and dominating Europe's seas. Louis achieved much in modernizing the French state but failed to control and centralize the economy, ensuring social upheaval and economic collapse for his successors. His revocation of the Edict of Nantes led to the flight of 200,000 Huguenots and ended any hope of again enlisting the Protestant German states against the Habsburgs.

Britain, Spain, and the Ottomans

In 1714, the Protestant George I, Elector of Hanover, came to the British throne, keeping the Catholics from power and involving Britain deeply in European politics for the remainder of the century. The deposed Stuart royal family became a focus for political discontent for several decades.

The War of the Spanish Succession (1701–14) was fought on the death of the last Habsburg king of Spain, which was now little more than a battleground for foreign armies. Britain, Holland, and the Austrian Habsburgs lined up against the Bourbons, who claimed the throne with French backing. The Bourbons were successful, despite several major French defeats.

After a series of reforms under Kara Mustafa, the Ottomans advanced a huge army against Vienna in 1683, but the city was relieved by a German and Polish army. Austrian Habsburg forces swiftly reconquered Hungary, before Turkish resistance stiffened.

Revocation
The taking back, or revoking, of a law.

Elector
One of the German princes entitled to take part in choosing the Holy Roman emperor.

European Economy

The 16th to 18th centuries saw population and city growth, the introduction of sophisticated financial systems, and innovations in farming and industry.

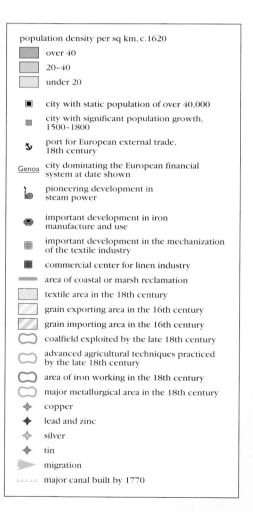

population density per sq km, c.1620

- over 40
- 20–40
- under 20

- ■ city with static population of over 40,000
- ■ city with significant population growth, 1500–1800
- ⚓ port for European external trade, 18th century
- <u>Genoa</u> city dominating the European financial system at date shown
- 🏺 pioneering development in steam power
- ⚙ important development in iron manufacture and use
- ▦ important development in the mechanization of the textile industry
- ▦ commercial center for linen industry
- — area of coastal or marsh reclamation
- ▧ textile area in the 18th century
- ▨ grain exporting area in the 16th century
- ▨ grain importing area in the 16th century
- ⬭ coalfield exploited by the late 18th century
- ⬭ advanced agricultural techniques practiced by the late 18th century
- ⬭ area of iron working in the 18th century
- ⬭ major metallurgical area in the 18th century
- ◆ copper
- ◆ lead and zinc
- ◇ silver
- ◆ tin
- ▶ migration
- ⌐⌐⌐ major canal built by 1770

Falkirk
Carron Iron Works, 1762
Edinburgh
1765
Newcastle
Bury
Kay, 1738   Hull
Manchester
Cromford
Arkwright, 1771   King's Lynn
Birmingham
Norwich
Bristol
oton
London
from 1763
La Havre
Amiens
Rouen
Huguenots
Paris
Passy
May/Meeres, 1726
Orléans
Troyes
Canal d'Orléans, 1692
Poitiers
Huguenots
Bordeaux
Huguenots
Toulouse
Montpellier
Aigues-
Mortes
Marseille
Nice
Barcelona
Palma
Balearic
Islands

*North
Sea*

Stockholm
Vänern
Vättern
Swedes
Copenhagen
Königsberg
Vilna
Danzig
*Baltic
Sea*
Lübeck
Hamburg   Stettin
Elbe–Oder canal,
1745
Bremen   Berlin   *Poles*
Vistula   *Poles*
Warsaw
Amsterdam
1627–1783
Deventer
Minden
Rotterdam   Bielefeld   Breslau
Middelburg   Elderfeld
Bruges   Antwerp   Cologne   Krakow
Ghent   1501–68   Leipzig
Brussels
Lille   Jemappe   Liège   Lemberg
Cambrai   1729
Valenciennes   Frankfurt   Prague
Péronne
St Quentin   Nuremberg   *Serbs*
Strasbourg   Augsburg   *Danube*   Vienna
Rhine   Ravensburg   Salzburg   Buda
St Gallen
Geneva   *Swiss*   *Serbs*
Lyon   *Swiss*   *Swiss*   Trieste
Vaucanson, 1742   Brescia
Milan   Verona
Turin   Cremona   Venice
Po   1378–1510
Genoa   Bologna
1557–1627
Pisa   Florence
Livorno   Ancona   Sofia
Piombino
Corsica   Rome   *Serbs*
Naples   *Albanians*
Thessalonica
Albanians
Sardinia   Cagliari   Crotone
Athens
Mediterranean   Sea   Palermo   Messina
Sicily

European Economy

Europe's economy in 1783 still rested on a base of semisubsistence agriculture, poor transport, local economies based partly on barter, lack of development capital, and the slow adoption of technological advances. Important developments in agriculture, industry, and commerce had taken place since the 16th century, but their social impact was still slight.

Population growth in the 16th century put pressure on resources, resulting in rising prices and falling wages. Population stagnation in the 17th century allowed a slight rise in living standards, but renewed population growth in the later 18th century was not matched by an increase in production and brought renewed hardship. Overall, Europe's population doubled between 1500 and 1800. The cities grew most: London and Paris exceeded 250,000 inhabitants by 1700.

Sophisticated finance

In the cities, a higher level of economic activity took place. Sophisticated banking and credit systems emerged, providing finance not only for long-distance trade but also for monarchs and governments. This new merchant capitalism made possible Europe's transformation into the world's economic powerhouse.

After 1492, the economic area dependent on European capitalism reached across the Atlantic to incorporate the Americas and spread a galaxy of trading bases across south and east Asia. Its center of gravity, having see-sawed between Flanders and northern Italy, finally settled at Amsterdam in the 17th century and London in the late 18th. A succession of financially dominant cities took European capitalism progressively closer to world domination. Britain's precocious national economy centered on London finally proved too powerful for its predecessors.

North–south rivalry

In the late 15th century, the dominant financial powers were Venice and the Hanseatic League, each controlling a network of trade routes. Flemish and English incursions into Hanseatic areas, and the arrival of Portuguese ships with East Indies spices at Antwerp, resulted in their collapse. From 1501 to 1568, European capitalism was dominated by the bankers of Antwerp. The distribution of American silver was handled from Flanders, while Dutch and Flemish ships dominated the Baltic grain trade to southern Europe. In 1557, the first Spanish state bankruptcy damaged the Antwerp banking system. For the next seventy years, Europe's finances were managed from Genoa.

As silver from Spanish America reduced, Amsterdam emerged as Europe's financial powerhouse in the 1620s. Maritime expertise combined with a stable, subtle, and flexible credit system led to Dutch control of much European and Asian trade. Britain and France made strenuous efforts to compete. The advantages of a stable banking system and an established system of national debt finally told in Britain's favor.

Background to the Industrial Revolution

New agricultural techniques in the 18th century—the enclosure of common land, improved crop rotation and animal husbandry, and the drainage of marginal lands—spread across Britain and the Netherlands. Transportation was revolutionized by the construction of canal networks, and energy use by the exploitation of coalfields. The steam engine, which was developed in 1712 in England to pump water from coal and tin mines, was turned into a source of mechanical power in 1776. Metallurgy was also revolutionized in England, and the mechanization of the textile industry led to the first modern-style factories—and the beginnings of what became known as the Industrial Revolution.

Bankruptcy
The legal state of being financially ruined.

Curriculum Context

Many curricula ask students to describe the characteristics of the agricultural revolution in western Europe and analyze its effects on population growth, industrialization, and patterns of land-holding.

Russian Expansion

In the 18th century, the formerly isolated Russian empire adopted western European ideas and became involved in European politics and trade.

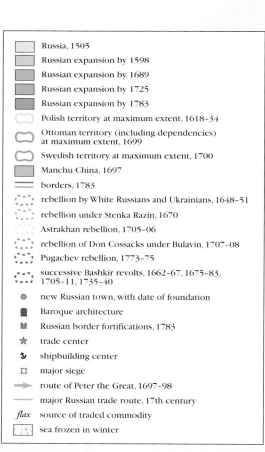

Russia, 1505

Russian expansion by 1598

Russian expansion by 1689

Russian expansion by 1725

Russian expansion by 1783

Polish territory at maximum extent, 1618–34

Ottoman territory (including dependencies) at maximum extent, 1699

Swedish territory at maximum extent, 1700

Manchu China, 1697

borders, 1783

rebellion by White Russians and Ukrainians, 1648–51

rebellion under Stenka Razin, 1670

Astrakhan rebellion, 1705–06

rebellion of Don Cossacks under Bulavin, 1707–08

Pugachev rebellion, 1773–75

successive Bashkir revolts, 1662–67, 1675–83, 1705–11, 1735–40

● new Russian town, with date of foundation

Baroque architecture

Russian border fortifications, 1783

★ trade center

shipbuilding center

major siege

➡ route of Peter the Great, 1697–98

— major Russian trade route, 17th century

flax source of traded commodity

sea frozen in winter

Barents Sea

Saami

Samoyeds

Obdorsk 1595

Berezov 1593

Surgut 1594

Ob

Nenets

Voguls

Archangel 1583

Yarensk

Pelym 1592

Tobolsk 1587

gems, silk, tea from Siberia and China

to Europe

Karelia 1617–1721 to Sweden

Lake Onega

flax, furs, hemp, potash, tallow, timber

Ustyug

Solikamskaya

Verkhotyure 1598

Tyumen 1586

Ishim 1670

Irtysh

furs to Siberia and China

Ingria 1617–1721 to Sweden

St Petersburg 1703

Olonets

Kargopol

furs, gems, silk, tea

Vyatka

Yegoshika (Perm)

Omsk 1716

ea, textiles, cco, wine stern Europe

Helsingfors (Helsinki)

Revel

Narva 1700

Tsarskoye Selo

Eastern Dvina

Vologda

Volyaks

Ufa 1586

Bashkirs

DEN

Estonia

Lake Peipus

Pskov

Novgorod

flax, grain, hides, iron, timber

Yaroslavl

Volga

Kazan Tatars

Kazan

Kirghiz

Livonia

Riga

Libau

Western Dvina

Pskov

Tver

Nizhniy Novgorod

Simbirsk 1648

Moscow

Ural Cossacks

Orenburg 1743

Oral

Königsberg June–July 1697

Vitebsk

Smolensk

Mogilev

Tula

Tambov 1636

Kazakhs

Minsk

Orel 1564

Saratov 1590

Turgay

POLAND

Ukraine

Voronezh 1586

to Poland 1618/34–1667/86

Kiev

Don

Tsaritsyn 1589

Nogai Tatars

Guryev 1645

Uzbegs

Warsaw

Kharkov 1654

Poltava 1709

Dnieper

Don Cossacks

Astrakhan Tatars

Krakow

Lemberg (Lvov)

Podolia

Zaporogian Cossacks

Astrakhan

Aral Sea

AUSTRIAN EMPIRE

Jassy

Stanilasti 1711

Kinburn

Azov 1695, 1696, 1736

KHANATE OF CRIMEA

arms, hardware, textiles to Persia

Amu Darya

Khiva

Danube

Kaffa

Kerch

Terek Cossacks

Volga

gems, silk from Persia

Derbent

Turkomans

Sevastopol 1783

Black Sea

CAUCASUS MTS

Georgia

Tiflis

1723–32 to Russia

Baku

Caspian Sea

Varna

Batum

Constantinople

Yerevan

Gorgan

Meshed

OTTOMAN EMPIRE

Tabriz

Tehran

PERSIA

Baghdad

Russian Expansion

By the late 15th century, the Grand Principality of Muscovy was deeply isolated. The fall of Constantinople to the Ottomans in 1453 left the Russian church the only significant Orthodox alternative to Catholicism, and their long struggle against the Tatars had convinced the Russians that western Europe had survived the last great nomad onslaught at Muscovy's expense.

Ivan III of Muscovy ended the independence of its rival Novgorod in 1478. Two years later, Muscovy finally threw off the Tatar yoke.

The reign of Ivan the Terrible

Khanate

A state composed of Turkish, Tatar, or Mongol tribes, ruled by a khan.

Boyar

A Russian high noble, ranked below a ruling prince.

Ivan IV the Terrible oversaw the Russian conquest of the Tatar khanates of Kazan and Astrakhan from 1552, opening trade routes down the Volga to the Caspian and through the southern Urals toward central Asia. To the west, he struck toward the Baltic but in the resulting Livonian War (1558–82), Sweden, Denmark, and Poland all intervened against Russia. Lacking the resources for a professional army and unable to rely on the semi-independent boyars, Ivan converted the former Novgorod lands to a personal fee, dispossessing the boyars and redistributing their estates to a nobility entirely dependent on the czar. All remaining free peasant communities were destroyed. In the resulting civil war, a Crimean Tatar army sacked Moscow.

Troubles and rebellions

By 1595, Russian control over Pskov and eastern Ukraine was secure, but further progress to the north or west was impossible. Incursions by other European powers continued during the Time of Troubles (1604–13): Poland and Sweden intervened in the civil war that devastated much of western Russia. The first of several huge rebellions shook southern Russia in 1670, but with no independent nobility to support them and little tradition of local autonomy (self-government), all were overcome, while a rebellion of the Don and Dnieper Cossacks against Poland allowed Russia to extend its frontiers south to the Ottoman client state of the Crimea and as far west as Kiev.

Modernization, industry, and expansion

The defining moment in Russian history came at the end of the century. Peter I the Great rejected traditional Russian antagonism to the West and traveled to Europe in 1697–98 in pursuit of ideas, technology, and assistance in modernizing his empire. By 1721, the power of Russia's deadliest northern rival, Sweden, had been broken, the trading ports of the eastern Baltic were in Russian hands, and Peter's new capital, Saint Petersburg, had risen from the Neva marshes to attract French culture and English and Dutch trade. Large state-run iron and copper industries grew up in the Urals in the 18th century, along with a vast armory at Tula and shipyards elsewhere.

Client state

A state that is dependent on another country economically, militarily, or politically.

Curriculum Context

Accounting for the growth of bureaucratic monarchy in Russia and analyzing the significance of Peter the Great's reforms are highlighted in many world history curricula.

Fur traders

Russian traders pursued furs across northern Asia, brushing aside the tiny native communities and establishing a series of trading fairs in southern Siberia. Official trade was highly regulated, but huge quantities of furs and other goods were traded illicitly to central Asia and China. Russian pioneers reached the Pacific coast by 1637 but were forced out of the Amur basin in 1689. By 1800, they had established a string of fur-trading posts and forts in Russian America (Alaska).

Through the 18th century, Russian armies gradually drove the Ottomans from the Crimea and southern Ukraine, opening the Black Sea to Russian trade. The czar's new status as a major player in European politics also involved Russia in new wars: its participation in the Seven Years' War almost destroyed Prussia, while Russia, Austria, and Prussia partitioned Poland in 1772.

The Ancien Régime

The 18th century saw the Netherlands, France, and Britain struggle for world dominance, and Austria and Prussia compete to take the place of the Holy Roman empire.

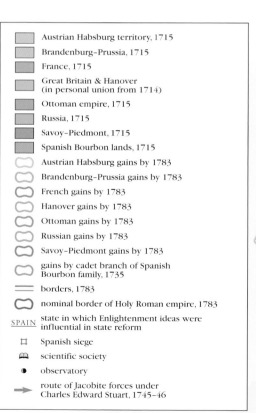

▨	Austrian Habsburg territory, 1715
▨	Brandenburg-Prussia, 1715
▨	France, 1715
▨	Great Britain & Hanover (in personal union from 1714)
▨	Ottoman empire, 1715
▨	Russia, 1715
▨	Savoy-Piedmont, 1715
▨	Spanish Bourbon lands, 1715
◠	Austrian Habsburg gains by 1783
◠	Brandenburg-Prussia gains by 1783
◠	French gains by 1783
◠	Hanover gains by 1783
◠	Ottoman gains by 1783
◠	Russian gains by 1783
◠	Savoy-Piedmont gains by 1783
◠	gains by cadet branch of Spanish Bourbon family, 1735
=	borders, 1783
◠	nominal border of Holy Roman empire, 1783
SPAIN	state in which Enlightenment ideas were influential in state reform
⌂	Spanish siege
📖	scientific society
●	observatory
→	route of Jacobite forces under Charles Edward Stuart, 1745–46

Map labels:
Culloden 1746; Scotland; Glasgow; Edinburgh 1739; Preston 1745; Ireland; Dublin 1731; GREAT BRITAIN; York; Wales; Derby; Birmingham 1766; England; Bristol; London 1660; Caen 1705; R; Brest; Pa; Quiberon Bay 1759; Loire; Nantes; Clermont Ferr; SARD; Bordeaux 1712; La Coruña; Santander; Bilbao; Pamplona; Toulo 1782; Douro; Oporto; Madrid 1713, 1738; Tagus; SPAIN; Valencia; Bar; 1782; PORTUGAL; Lisbon 1779; Guadiana; Balearic Islands; Córdoba; Cartagena; Seville; Lagos 1759; Cádiz; Gibraltar to Britain 1779–83

Christiania

SWEDEN

Uppsala
1710

Vänern

Göteborg

Vättern

Gotland

DENMARK–NORWAY

Stockholm
1741

Baltic Sea

Copenhagen
1742

Karelia
1721 to Russia

St Petersburg
1724

Helsingfors
(Helsinki)

Ingria
1721 to Russia

Revel

Estonia
1721 to Russia

Novgorod

*Lake
Peipus*

Moscow

Livonia
1721 to Russia

Riga

Courland

Western Drina

Polish Livonia
1772 to Russia

Smolensk

RUSSIA

West Pomerania
1720 to Brandenburg–Prussia

Bremen–Verden
1715 to Hanover

Königsberg

Danzig

PRUSSIA

SERREY

Lithuania

White
Russia
1772 to Russia

Gomel

East Friesland
Brandenburg–Prussia

West
Prussia
1772 to
Brandenburg–
Prussia

Minsk

NETHERLANDS

Minden
1759

HANOVER

Göttingen
1736

BRANDENBURG

Potsdam

Berlin
1700

Zorndorf
1758

Great
Poland

Warsaw

Ermland
1772 to Brandenburg–Prussia

Oder

POLAND

Kiev

Kharkov

Brussels
1772

Cologne

Leipzig

SAXONY

Silesia
1742 to Brandenburg–
Prussia

Lublin

Volhynia

Ukraine

Dnieper

Netherlands

Frankfurt

Rossbach
1757

Dresden

Leuthen
1757

Mollwitz
1741

Vistula

Krakow

Galicia &
Lodomeria
1772 to Austria

Podolia

**Zaporogian
Cossacks**

Dettingen
1743

Prague

Bohemia

Moravia

Nuremberg

Mannheim
1755

BAVARIA

Austria

Vienna

Danube

AUSTRIAN EMPIRE

Bukovina
1775 to
Austria

Jassy

Jedisan

1774 to
Russia

ncy
1736

Munich
1759

Styria

Buda

Hungary

MOLDAVIA

ion
723

Carinthia

Mohács

**KHANATE OF
CRIMEA**
1783 to Russia

ne

Bern

**SWISS
CONFEDERATION**

Carniola

Peterwardein
1716

Banat
1718 to Austria

Serbia
1718–39 to
Austria

WALLACHIA

eva
776

VENICE

Sava

Lesser
Wallachia
1718–39 to
Austria

Bucharest

MILAN

Padua
1779

Venice
1779

Bosnia

Danube

NT
718
714/48 to
–Piedmont

Turin
1757

Genoa

PARMA
1731 to Spain,
1733 to Austria,
1748 to Spain

Varna

Black Sea

GENOA

Marseille
1726

TUSCANY
1737 to Austria

Florence
1752

PAPAL STATES

MONTENEGRO

Bulgaria

Adrianople

Constantinople

**STATO DEI
PRESIDII**
1737 to Spain

Rome

Uskub

OTTOMAN

Thessalonica

Albania

ANATOLIA

Corsica
1768/69 to
France

BENEVENTO

NAPLES
1735 to Spain

Naples
1779

Taranto

Janina

EMPIRE

32

SARDINIA
1720 to Sardinia–
Piedmont

Chesmé
1770

Izmir

Cagliari

Athens

SICILY
1720 to Austria,
1735 to Spain

Palermo

Morea
1718 to
Ottoman
empire

*Mediterranean
Sea*

MALTA

The Ancien Régime

In 1713, the Treaty of Utrecht partitioned the former Spanish Habsburg territories between the Bourbons and Austrian Habsburgs and confirmed that no single empire controlled the affairs of Europe. A new concept emerged of the balance of power.

Ancien régime

A term for the old political and social systems prevalent in Europe up to the end of the 18th century, in which monarchs, clergy, and aristocrats were dominant.

Curriculum Context

Students can demonstrate the influence of ideas on events by explaining the principal ideas of the Enlightenment, such as rationalism, secularism, toleration, contractual government, and new theories of education.

Serfdom

The state of being a serf, having to work on the land and be subject to the will of the land's owner.

Yet the Europe of the ancien régime was still a network of dynastic states, with little effective representation in government by financial or mercantile groups, except in Britain and the Netherlands.

Enlightenment ideas

Western Europe now began a period of economic growth. The religious wars of the 17th century had turned many people toward natural philosophy (science), which seemed to offer a surer route than faith to peace and harmony. The spread of academies of science and observatories and new movements in art, architecture, and music were manifestations of the Enlightenment. Influential thinkers such as Voltaire questioned assumptions about social order and sought a new, rational basis for human affairs. This mainly aristocratic intellectual elite tried to persuade dynastic rulers to remodel society, including the ending of judicial torture and the abolition of serfdom.

Prosperity and poverty

Rising population and economic growth brought prosperity for some but hardship for many. Where serfdom survived, rising prices, falling wages, and poor agricultural techniques increased social tensions. Even where agricultural yields improved, the beneficiaries were merchants, financiers, and industrialists rather than the majority employed in agricultural production.

Opposing the Ottomans

Relative peace in central and northeastern Europe allowed the rulers of Austria and Russia to concentrate on domestic reform and the struggle to roll back the Ottomans. The Habsburgs rebuilt their authority in the Holy Roman empire and extended their sway in Hungary. Russia pushed south, and its Baltic fleet destroyed the Ottoman fleet at Chesmé.

A time of wars

From mid-century a new series of dynastic wars overtook Europe, exacerbated by a worldwide conflict between the Netherlands, France, and Britain. In the case of Poland (1733–35), a proxy war between France, Spain, Savoy, and Austria was largely fought in Italy. Poland itself was left entirely dominated by Austria and Russia, its decline finally confirmed by the First Partition in 1772. The Holy Roman empire was swept away in 1740, with the opening of a 130-year struggle for dominance between Austria and Prussia, newly promoted to the rank of great power through the policies and reforms of Frederick William I. His son, Frederick the Great, wrested Silesia from the Habsburgs. Louis XV, allied to Prussia, suffered a defeat at British-Hanoverian hands at Dettingen but overran the Austrian Netherlands after defeating a British army at Fontenoy.

Maria Theresa of Austria sought revenge in the Seven Years' War, allied with France and Russia against Prussia and Britain. Despite a string of victories, Frederick of Prussia was saved only by the withdrawal of Russia from the alliance against him. An Anglo-Brunswick victory at Minden saved Hanover from French invasion; British naval supremacy was restored by victories over the French at Lagos and Quiberon Bay; Britain also overran French North America. Louis XVI had a chance for revenge when Britain's American colonies rebelled, but French participation in the American victory caused a financial crisis. By contrast, Britain's strength was underlined in the last Anglo-Dutch War, climaxing at the battle of Dogger Bank in 1782.

Proxy war

A war fought over a country that itself does not take part in the war.

Curriculum Context

The Seven Years' War, Enlightenment thought, the American Revolution, and a growing internal economic crisis all affected social and political conditions in France.

The Rise of the Ottoman Empire

The Islamic Turkish Ottoman state expanded in the second half of the 15th century to become one of the world's greatest empires.

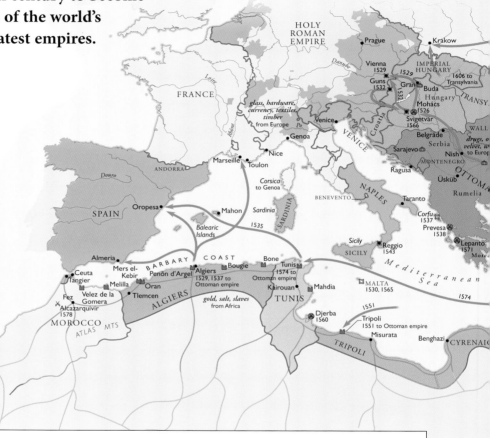

Map labels include:

HOLY ROMAN EMPIRE · Prague · Krakow · Vienna 1529 · 1529 · IMPERIAL HUNGARY · 1606 to Transylvania · Guns 1532 · Gran · 1532 · Buda · TRANSY. · Hungary · Mohács 1526 · Svigetvár 1566 · WALL · Belgrade · Serbia · drugs, velvet, to Europe · Sarajevo · Nish · MONTENEGRO · OTTO · FRANCE · glass, hardware, currency, textiles, timber from Europe · Venice · Po · Genoa · VENICE · Croatia · Ragusa · Üsküb · Rumelia · Loire · Nice · Marseille · Toulon · ANDORRA · Corsica to Genoa · BENEVENTO · NAPLES · Taranto · Douro · Oropesa · Mahon · Sardinia · SARDINIA · Corfu 1537 · Prevesa 1538 · SPAIN · Balearic Islands · 1535 · Sicily · Reggio 1543 · SICILY · Lepanto 1571 · Morea · Almeria · BARBARY COAST · Bone · Tunis 1574 to Ottoman empire · Mediterranean Sea · Ceuta · Tangier · Mers el-Kebir · Penõn d'Argel · Algiers 1529, 1537 to Ottoman empire · Bougie · Melilla · Oran · Kairouan · Mahdia · MALTA 1530, 1565 · 1574 · Fez · Velez de la Gomera · Tlemcen · ALGIERS · gold, salt, slaves from Africa · TUNIS · 1551 · Alcazarquivir 1578 · MOROCCO · ATLAS MTS · Djerba 1560 · Tripoli 1551 to Ottoman empire · Misurata · Benghazi · CYRENAI · TRIPOLI · Danube

Legend

- Ottoman empire, 1492
- Ottoman conquests by 1520
- Ottoman conquests, 1520–66
- Ottoman conquests, 1566–1640
- Habsburg territory, 1550
- Venetian territory, 1550
- Safavid territory, 1512
- Safavid territory conquered by Ottomans but regained before 1640
- Crimean Tatar territory lost to Zaporogian Cossacks before 1640
- Ottoman administrative center
- Ottoman victory
- Ottoman defeat
- Ottoman siege
- ☆ center for Ottoman trade with Europe
- Spanish *presidio* fort
- Spanish *presidio* fort captured by Ottomans
- *gems* trade commodity in the Ottoman empire
- → Ottoman/Tatar campaign or raid
- — trade route

RUSSIA

Moscow

Kazan

Volga

Cossacks

1571–72

Dnieper

1521

Kiev

Ukraine

Podolia

VIA

Jedisan

Akkerman

grain to Constantinople

1538

hardware, textiles from Europe and Russia

Kaffa

1527, 1543

Astrakhan

Azov

KHANATE OF THE CRIMEA

1579–80

CAUCASUS MTS

Derbent

Caspian Sea

Black Sea

carpets, gems, skins, tobacco to Europe and Russia

Batum

Georgia

Tiflis

Shirvan

Baku 1583 to Ottoman empire

harest

Varna

Sinope

Trabzon

Samsun

Kars

Yerevan

Armenia

1578

Azerbaijan

Edirne (Adrianople)

Amasra

antinople

Scutari

Ankara

Tokat

Sivas

ZAGROS

silk from Asia

Bursa

Kayseri

Chaldiran 1514

Tabriz 1514 to Ottoman empire

Hamadan

SAFAVID EMPIRE

EMPIRE

ANATOLIA

Diyarbakir

Mardin

i

Izmir

Konya

Tarsus

Adana

Urfa

Kurdistan

Mosul

MESOPOTAMIA

Luristan

PERSIA

Rhodes 1522

Iskanderun

Marj Dabiq 1516

Qasr-i-Shirin

ZAGROS

drugs, gems, spices to Europe

Aleppo 1516 to Ottoman empire

Euphrates

Tigris

dia

Famagusta 1571

Syria

ete

Cyprus 1571 to Ottoman empire

Tripoli

Baghdad 1534 to Ottoman empire

MTS

Damascus 1516 to Ottoman empire

Iraq

rugs, gems, spices o Constantinople and Europe

Jerusalem

Desert Route

Basra 1546 to Ottoman empire

currency from Europe

Bandar Abbas 1551

Gaza

Alexandria

al-Raydaniyya 1517

Suez

Hormuz 1514–1622 to Portugal

Cairo 1517 to Ottoman empire

Egypt

El Hasa

Bahrain 1554

gems, rice, spices from southeast Asia

Muscat 1551

Asyut

currency to Asia

Quseir

Nile

Arabs

OMAN

Darb al-Arabain

El Kharga

Aswan

Medina

Selima

Jiddah

Mecca 1517 to Ottoman empire

Red Sea

Suakin

drugs, gems, gold, slaves, spices from Asia and Africa

FUNJ

Massawa

Sana

YEMEN

ETHIOPIA

Mocha

Aden 1538 to Ottoman empire

The Rise of the Ottoman Empire

The rise of the Ottoman Turkish state from a regional power in Asia Minor in the mid-15th century to the greatest empire in Europe and West Asia by the mid-16th was a dramatic one. In less than a century, the house of Osman had destroyed Byzantium and become leaders of the Islamic world, ruling an empire stretching from the Atlas Mountains to the Caspian Sea.

Curriculum Context

The capture of Constantinople in 1453 and the destruction of the Byzantine empire contributed greatly to the expansion of Ottoman power and was a hugely symbolic blow against Europe's dominance.

A key moment in this transformation was the capture of Constantinople by Mehmet II in 1453. Then between 1516 and 1520, the armies of Selim I (r.1512–20) drove the Safavid Persians out of Kurdistan, destroyed the empire of the Mamlukes, and secured recognition by Mecca of their sultan as caliph, or leader of the Islamic faithful. The conquest of Syria and Egypt from the Mamlukes made the Ottoman territories part of a vast network of caravan routes from Morocco to the gates of Beijing. At one end of this network were the spices, drugs, silks, and (later) porcelain of the east; at the other, the traders in gold dust, slaves, gems, and other products of Africa and the shipments of textiles, glass, hardware, timber, and currency from Europe.

The Ottomans in Europe

In Christian Europe, Francis I of France allied himself with Suleiman the Magnificent (r.1520–66) against the Habsburgs. Suleiman reduced Hungary to vassal status after his victory at Mohács in 1526, then conquered a swathe of European territory from Croatia to the Black Sea. Ultimately, however, the Ottomans' religious war with Safavid Persia saved Habsburg central Europe.

Vassal status

Having to obey another state in return for protection.

Ottoman–Christian frontiers

The Ottoman–Christian frontier on the Danube achieved a kind of equilibrium after the death of Suleiman. In the Mediterranean, Ottoman conquest of the North African coast was facilitated by the naval victory at Prevesa, but Charles V's offensive at Tunis (1535) and the Christian victory at Lepanto (1571) restored the status quo: a rough division of the sea along a line through Italy, Sicily, and Tunisia.

Ottoman setbacks

The most costly of the Ottoman–Safavid wars broke out in 1602; the reorganized and reequipped armies of the Persians reversed almost all the Ottoman gains of the previous century before a peace was agreed. Constantinople was devastated by plagues and economic crises. The empire was further weakened by the lack of a clear custom of succession and by the growing independence and political influence of the Janissaries. These were originally an elite military and administrative caste recruited from children of Balkan Christians, who were surrendered as tribute to Constantinople. This caste increasingly played the role of the empire's kingmakers. From the mid-century, too, the caravan routes' profitability began to wane under pressure from alternative routes to East Asia. By 1640, the Ottoman empire was falling behind its European rivals in military technology, wealth, and political unity.

Curriculum Context

In some states, students are asked to analyze reasons for Ottoman military successes against Persia, Egypt, North African states, and Christian European kingdoms.

Caste

A social class with its own occupations and restrictions.

Trade between Europe and Asia

The wars between Ottomans and Christians never entirely halted trade between Europe and Asia. European merchant ships continued to arrive at Iskanderun or Tripoli in Syria, or at Alexandria, and to unload cargoes of European goods and quantities of Spanish–American gold and silver destined for Asia. These cargoes were carried through the Ottoman and Safavid empires in caravans forbidden to Europeans. These caravans were meticulously organized, secure, regular, and often faster than the European sea routes. They brought Asian goods back for export to Europe from Mediterranean ports. Until the mid-17th century, this trade flourished, enriching the Ottoman empire and making European technology available to the sultan.

The Decline of the Ottoman Empire

From the mid 17th century
to the end of the 19th, the
Ottomans struggled to hold
their empire together in a
series of military campaigns.

N

ESTONIA

Libau

Venta PRUSSIA

Warsaw

POLA

1672 to Ott
16

Prague

Krakow   Galicia

HOLY ROMAN
EMPIRE   *Danube*

AUSTRIAN EMPIR

Vienna
1683   ⊗ 1686
Buda   TRANSYLVAN
1699 to Austria
empire

AUSTRIA
St Gotthard
1644   Hungary   1699 to Austrian empire

FRANCE

Mohács
1687   Zenta
1697

Peterwardein
1716   Slankamen
169   W
1718 to
1739 re

Venice   Karlowitz   Belgrade

Loire   Serbia

Po   Karlowitz   Nish
1689

Sarajevo

VENICE

Rhône

TUSCANY   MONTENEGRO
1699 independent   OTTO

RAGUSA
1718 independent   Üsküb

ANDORRA   Corsica
to Genoa

Douro   Corfu
1716

Rumelia

Benevento   NAPLES

SPAIN   Sardinia   Corinth
1715

Balearic
Islands   SARDINIA   1685–99 to Venice,
1718 regained by Ottoman
empire   Morea

Sicily   Coron
1685

Algiers   Bone   *Mediterranean*   SICILY
Bougie   Tunis
Sea

Ceuta   Mahdia   MALTA
Tangier   ALGIERS
Melilla   c.1610 semi-independent

Tlemcen

Fez   c.1714 semi-
independent   c.1714 semi-
independent

MOROCCO   TUNIS
c.1705 semi-
independent   Tripoli   independent
Misurata   Benghazi   CYRENAI
TRIPOLI

Marrakech

▨ Ottoman empire, 1640		▬ restored Ottoman–Persia border, 1747	
▨ Ottoman gains after 1640		═ borders, 1783	
⌢ Ottoman gains that were subsequently lost		⊗ Ottoman victory	
⌢ Ottoman territories effectively independent by 1783		⊗ Ottoman defeat	
▨ Safavid territory, 1640		⊡ Ottoman siege	
▨ Habsburg territory, 1640		⊡ Russian siege	
▨ Austrian Habsburg territory, 1783		— Armenian merchant route	
▨ Russian empire, 1689		— main pilgrimage route to Mecca	
▨ Russian gains by 1783			
▨ Venetian territory, 1783			
▨ area of Wahhabi influence by c.1783			

RUSSIA
Novgorod
Nizhniy Novgorod
Kazan
Volga
Moscow
Vitebsk
molensk
Kiev
Dnieper
odolia
Astrakhan
Jedisan
Azov
1687, 1689
Stanilasti
1711
Akkerman
KHANATE OF
THE CRIMEA
1783 to Russian empire
Kaffa
Derbent
CAUCASUS MTS
Caspian Sea
Georgia
Batum
Tiflis
(Tbilisi)
Baku
Shirvan
Black Sea
Varna
Sinope
Trabzon
1745
Yerevan
Azerbaijan
tari
Amasra
Samsun
Kars
Armenia
ntinople
Tokat
Tehran
Bursa
Ankara
Sivas
1730 lost by Ottomans
1747 regained
Tabriz
EMPIRE
ANATOLIA
Kayseri
Diyarbekir
Kurdistan
Z
Konya
Adana
Urfa
Mardin
Mosul
A
Izmir
Kütahya
Tarsus
Hamadan
Nehavend
1730
Isfahan
1727
G
PERSIA
Iskanderun
MESOPOTAMIA
R
hodes
Famagusta
Aleppo
Euphrates
Tigris
Luristan
O
ia
Cyprus
Syria
Baghdad
1735
S
Tripoli
Damascus
Iraq
M
toman empire
Jerusalem
Gaza
Basra
Shiraz
T
S
Alexandria
Suez
Cairo
Bandar Abbas
Hormuz
Egypt
Hejaz
El Hasa
BAHRAIN
1783 independent
Asyut
Quseir
QATAR
c.1780 independent
Muscat
Riyadh
OMAN
Aswan
Nile
Medina
1783 independent
NEJD
Jiddah
Mecca
Red Sea
Suakin
Massawa
Sana
1635 independent
FUNJ
YEMEN
Mocha
Aden
ETHIOPIA

The Decline of the Ottoman Empire

The decline of the Ottoman empire was a slow process, interrupted by periods of revival or stability. The signs of decay became more acute in the 17th and 18th centuries in protracted conflicts with Venice, the Holy League, and Russia. Economic and social difficulties also increased steadily. Nevertheless, in 1783, the empire still extended from the Balkans through Greece, Asia Minor, the Levant, and Egypt to the holy places of Islam.

Blockade
To deploy ships or troops to prevent supplies or reinforcements reaching an enemy state.

An unsuccessful Ottoman attempt in 1645 to occupy Crete was a sign of the empire's failing power. The fleet, mothballed earlier in the century, had been allowed to rot. A Venetian fleet blockaded the Dardanelles and threatened Constantinople itself in 1648. Sultan Ibrahim (r. 1640–48) was deposed by the Janissaries during the resulting political crisis.

The Köprülü viziers

Vizier
A high-ranking executive officer in a Muslim state.

The deposition of Ibrahim heralded a period of reform and revival under the Köprülüs, an Albanian dynasty who were to occupy the office of grand vizier to the sultans until the early 18th century. Mehmet Köprülü eventually brought the Cretan war to a successful conclusion, stabilized the Danube front against Austria, and annexed Podolia. In 1683, however, his successor Kara Mustafa mounted the empire's last challenge to Christian Europe, culminating in a new siege of Vienna. A concerted German and Polish response inflicted a crushing defeat on the Ottoman forces. Between 1684 and 1690, Austrian armies broke into Hungary and Transylvania, and the Venetians overran Morea (the Peloponnese).

In 1690, a new grand vizier, Mustafa Köprülü, restored the empire's fortunes in the Balkans, leading a counteroffensive that drove the Austrians back across the Danube and recovered Transylvania. The following year, however, Mustafa was killed in a major Ottoman defeat at Slankamen. By 1700, Azov had fallen to the Russians, Hungary and Transylvania had been ceded to the Habsburgs, and Podolia to Poland.

Economic decline

Economically, the empire's decline was hastened by the aggressive monopolization of Indian Ocean trade by the British and Dutch East India companies from the mid-17th century onward. Although Ottoman commerce with the east never dried up entirely, trade through the Red Sea and Persian Gulf dwindled as ever more Asian goods were carried around the Cape of Good Hope to Amsterdam or London. Moreover, the opening up of Siberia gave Russian and European traders a land route to China that bypassed routes through Ottoman and Safavid territories. The loss of its role as trade intermediary between Europe, Africa, and Asia reduced much Ottoman territory to an economic backwater. It also deprived the empire of access to the latest European military technology.

Curriculum Context

Assessing the effect of European commercial penetration on Ottoman society and government is part of many curricula.

Territorial losses in the 18th century

In 1711, an Ottoman victory over Peter the Great brought the recovery of Azov, but the period 1714–18 saw a revival of hostilities with Venice, with Austrian advances in Serbia. The collapse of Safavid power allowed an agreement with Russia to partition western Persia, but the counteroffensives of Nadir Shah after 1730 cost the empire its Mesopotamian and Transcaucasian provinces. The Ottomans soon felt the full weight of Russian expansion. A series of defeats after 1768 led to the final loss of the Crimea, while a Russian fleet commanded by British officers crushed the empire's navy at Chesmé in 1770. By the end of the 18th century, most outlying Ottoman territories were independent, and the empire of Suleiman the Magnificent had become a mid-ranking power, with limited influence outside West Asia.

Curriculum Context

Studies of the decline of the Ottoman empire should analyze why the empire was forced to retreat from the Balkans and the Black Sea region.

Asia and the Safavids

From 1500, the Safavid Persian empire flourished for 200 years, as nomadic Mongol and Turkic peoples frequently migrated in search of territory.

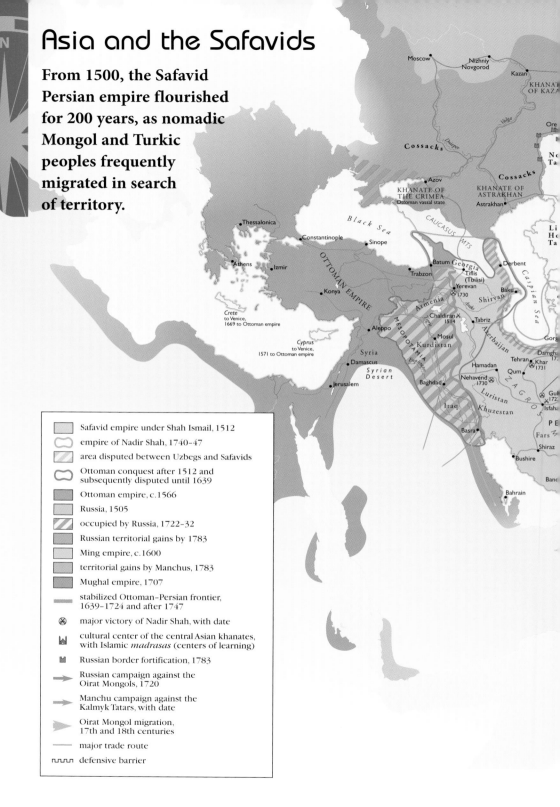

Safavid empire under Shah Ismail, 1512

empire of Nadir Shah, 1740–47

area disputed between Uzbegs and Safavids

Ottoman conquest after 1512 and subsequently disputed until 1639

Ottoman empire, c.1566

Russia, 1505

occupied by Russia, 1722–32

Russian territorial gains by 1783

Ming empire, c.1600

territorial gains by Manchus, 1783

Mughal empire, 1707

stabilized Ottoman–Persian frontier, 1639–1724 and after 1747

major victory of Nadir Shah, with date

cultural center of the central Asian khanates, with Islamic *madrasas* (centers of learning)

Russian border fortification, 1783

Russian campaign against the Oirat Mongols, 1720

Manchu campaign against the Kalmyk Tatars, with date

Oirat Mongol migration, 17th and 18th centuries

major trade route

defensive barrier

Moscow

Nizhniy Novgorod

Kazan

KHANATE OF KAZA

Volga

Ore

Cossacks

Dnieper

Azov

KHANATE OF THE CRIMEA
Ottoman vassal state

Cossacks

KHANATE OF ASTRAKHAN

Astrakhan

No Ta

Li He Ta

Thessalonica

Black Sea

Constantinople

Sinope

CAUCASUS MTS

Batum

Georgia

Tiflis (Tbilisi)

Derbent

Athens

Izmir

OTTOMAN EMPIRE

Trabzon

Yerevan

1730

Baku

Caspian Sea

Konya

Armenia

Araks

Shirvan

Crete
to Venice,
1669 to Ottoman empire

Chaldiran
1514

Tabriz

Azerbaijan

Gorg

Cyprus
to Venice,
1571 to Ottoman empire

Aleppo

MESOPOTAMIA

Mosul

Kurdistan

ZAGRO

Damgh
17

Syria

Tigris

Hamadan

Tehran

Khar
1731

Damascus

Syrian Desert

Euphrates

Baghdad

Nehavend
1730

Qum

Luristan

Khuzestan

Gul
172

Jerusalem

Iraq

Isfaha

Basra

PE

Fars

Shiraz

Bushire

Ban

Bahrain

RUSSIAN
EMPIRE

Verkhotyure
Tobolsk
Tyumen
KHANATE
OF SIBIR
Omsk

Tomsk

Buriats
SAYAN MOUNTAINS

Irkutsk
Kyakhta
Lake
Baykal

Ulan Bator
1696
1696

Mongolian
Steppe

Kirghiz

Semipalatinsk

Middle Horde Tatars

Golden
Horde
Tatars

Tarbagatai

Kabdo

ALTAI
MOUNTAINS

Oirat
Mongols

Gobi Desert
1755

Kazakhs

Lake
Balkhash

Kalmyk Tatars

Ili

DZUNGARIA

Hami

Khalka
Tatars

Ganzhou
Suzhou

Great Wall
1755-59

Aral
Sea

Kizil Kum

Yasi

Urumqi
Turfan

KHANATE OF
TURFAN

Lanzhou

Gansu

HANATE
F KHIVA
Khiva

TRANSOXIANA

Tashkent

Kokand

KHANATE OF
KASHGAR

TIEN SHAN

Aksu

Uzbegs

Samarkand
KHANATE OF
KOKAND

Kashgar

Bukhara
KHANATE OF
BUKHARA

Badakshan

FERGHANA

Yarkand

Khotan

Taklimakan Desert

KUNLUN MOUNTAINS

1510
Merv

HINDU
KUSH

Balkh

Khorasan
Meshed

KARAKORUM

Kashmir

LADAKH

Indus

Tibetan
Plateau

Kabul

Afghanistan

Peshawar

SAFAVID
EMPIRE
Herat
Seistan

Hilmand

Kandahar
1738

Punjab
Lahore

TIBET
1642 occupied by
Kalmyk Tatars

Brahmaputra

SIKKIM
Kathmandu

Kerman

Kerman

Baluchistan

Multan

Karnal
1739

Delhi

MUGHAL
EMPIRE

Thar Desert

Makran

Sind

Indus

Thatta

Muscat

Arabian
Sea

Asia and the Safavids

Between 1500 and 1800, Asia saw the rise and retrenchment of Safavid Persia, the expansion of Russia across Siberia, the emergence of powerful new states in Afghanistan and Manchu China, and the last nomad migrations in Eurasian history.

By 1500, most nomadic Turkic and Mongol peoples had been converted to Islam, and a number of Muslim khanates had emerged, in particular around the oasis-cities of the Silk Road. All these peoples were still feared by their settled neighbors for their capacity to expand explosively if their pastures became exhausted or economic circumstances worsened.

Nomads move eastward

In the early 15th century, the Ming Chinese had expelled the Mongols from their homeland north of the Great Wall and had then retired behind the Wall. Pressured by the rise of new empires in the west and Russian encroachment into the northern khanates of Kazan and Astrakhan, the nomads of central Asia moved east to fill this power vacuum from 1500.

Founding of the Mughal empire

As part of this eastward movement, the formidable Uzbegs expanded into Ferghana, homeland of the Turkic Mughals. Under Babur (r.1501–30), the Mughals established a base at Kabul, then crossed into northern India. Babur's subjugation of the Delhi sultanate led to the founding of the powerful Mughal empire.

Sultanate
A Muslim state governed by a sultan.

Safavid Persia

Safavid Persia grew rapidly under Shah Ismail (r.1501–24), expanding from Azerbaijan to occupy the area between the Caspian Sea and the Persian Gulf, and capturing Khorasan from the Uzbegs. This growth was halted by defeat at the hands of the Ottomans at Chaldiran in 1514. Seven decades of internal struggle and desperate defense against repeated invasions by the Uzbegs and Ottomans ensued. Under Shah Abbas the Great (r.1588–1629), however, Persia regained most of the lands lost to the Ottomans, took and held Kandahar against the Mughals, and prevailed over the Uzbegs in Khorasan. The Uzbegs now turned east, establishing the new khanate of Kokand. The Safavid empire survived until 1722, when it was overrun by the Afghans.

Curriculum Context

Studies of Safavid political and cultural achievements often focus on the reign of Shah Abbas, which is seen as Persia's golden age.

Manchu campaigns

In the early 17th century, the Manchus, a people of largely Mongol stock, crossed the Great Wall and overthrew Ming China in 1644. As in Mughal India, the invaders soon created a dynamic new state. In 1696, the Manchus destroyed the Oirat Mongol capital Ulan Bator, causing a westward migration. Harried by Manchu campaigns, the Oirats and Kalmyk Tatars destroyed the khanates of Dzungaria and pressed on to the lands around the Aral Sea.

Decline of the nomadic peoples

The Uzbeg khanates, impoverished by the decline of overland trade, faced a Persia revitalized by Nadir Shah (r.1736–47). Khiva, Afghanistan, and Balkh were lost; only Bukhara withstood the Persian onslaught.

Northward expansion of the Mongol peoples was held in check by the line of border forts that the Russians had established in Siberia. Initial conflict between Russia and Manchu China was resolved in a trade agreement that signaled the demise of the Silk Road.

Even the collapse of Persia could not restore nomad fortunes. A strong Afghan state emerged to dominate the lands south of Bukhara, while China extended its hegemony to the shores of Lake Balkhash by the end of the 18th century.

Hegemony

Influence or authority over others.

Sub-Saharan Africa

In this period, many important states emerged, and the transatlantic slave trade flourished.

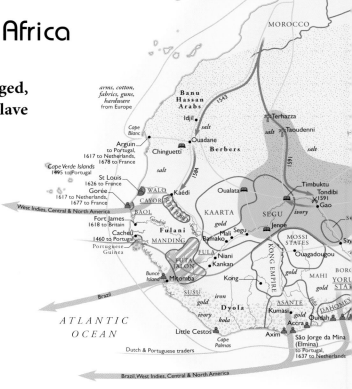

MOROCCO

arms, cotton, fabrics, guns, hardware from Europe

Banu Hassan Arabs

1543

Idjil · salt

Terhazza

Cape Blanc

Ouadane

Berbers

salt Taoudenni

Arguin
to Portugal,
1617 to Netherlands,
1678 to France

Chinguetti

salt

1591

Cape Verde Islands
1495 to Portugal

salt

1594

Timbuktu

St Louis
1626 to France

WALO

Kaédi

Oualata

Tondibi
×1591
· Gao

ivory

Gorée
1617 to Netherlands,
1677 to France

CAYOR

West Indies, Central & North America

BAOL

Gambia

KAARTA

SEGU

Fort James
1618 to Britain

Fulani

gold

Segu

Jenne

MOSSI
STATES

Say

Cacheu
1460 to Portugal

MANDING

Mali
Bamako

Portuguese
Guinea

FULA
· Niani

KONG EMPIRE

Ouagadougou

FUTA
JALON

· Kankan

gold

MAHI

BORG

Bunce
Island

Mitomba

Kong

gold

YORU
STAT

SUSU

iron

ASANTE

DAHOMEY

Brazil

gold

Dyola

Kumasi

gold

ivory

kola

Accra

Ouidah

ATLANTIC
OCEAN

Little Cestos

Cape
Palmas

Axim

São Jorge da Mina
(Elmina)
to Portugal,
1637 to Netherlands

Dutch & Portuguese traders

Brazil, West Indies, Central & North America

to Portugal, 1778

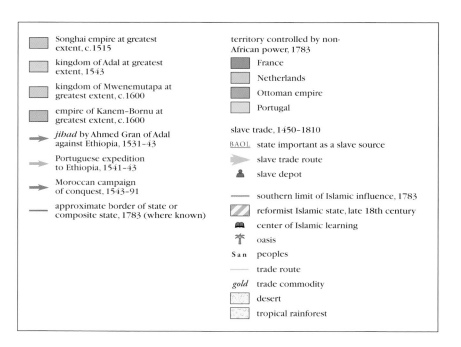

Songhai empire at greatest extent, c.1515	territory controlled by non-African power, 1783
kingdom of Adal at greatest extent, 1543	France
kingdom of Mwenemutapa at greatest extent, c.1600	Netherlands
empire of Kanem–Bornu at greatest extent, c.1600	Ottoman empire
jihad by Ahmed Gran of Adal against Ethiopia, 1531–43	Portugal

slave trade, 1450–1810

BAOL   state important as a slave source

→   slave trade route

Portuguese expedition to Ethiopia, 1541–43

Moroccan campaign of conquest, 1543–91

approximate border of state or composite state, 1783 (where known)

    slave depot

——   southern limit of Islamic influence, 1783

reformist Islamic state, late 18th century

center of Islamic learning

oasis

San   peoples

——   trade route

gold   trade commodity

desert

tropical rainforest

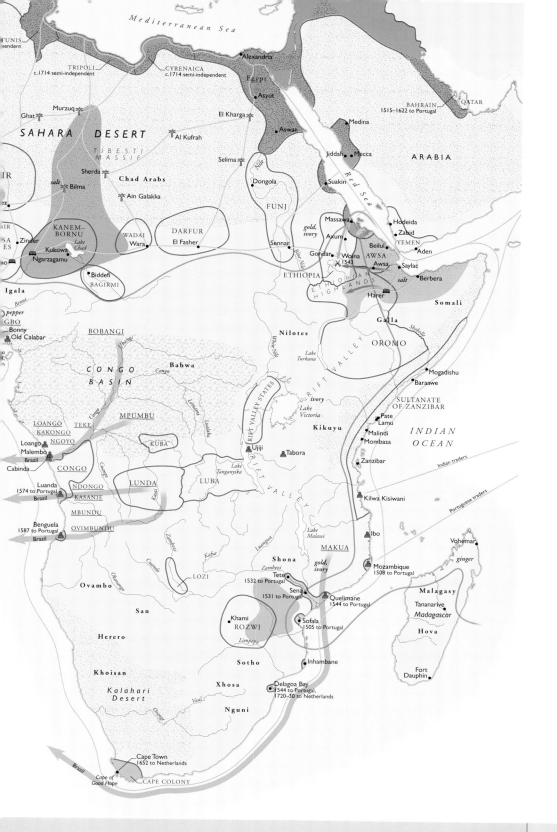

Mediterranean Sea

TUNIS
endent

TRIPOLI
c.1714 semi-independent

CYRENAICA
c.1714 semi-independent

Alexandria

Egypt

Asyut

El Kharga

Aswan

Ghat

Murzuq

SAHARA DESERT

TIBESTI MASSIF

Al Kufrah

Selima

Nile

Medina

Jiddah   Mecca

ARABIA

BAHRAIN
1515–1622 to Portugal

QATAR

IR

Sherda

Bilma   salt

Chad Arabs

Ain Galakka

Dongola

Suakin

Red Sea

Hodeida

Zabid

YEMEN

Aden

KANEM–
BORNU

WADAI
Wara

DARFUR
El Fasher

Sennar

FUNJ

Blue Nile

Massawa

Axum

Gondar   Wofla
1543

Beilul

AWSA
Awsa   salt   Saylac

Berbera

ez

Zinder

Kukuwa
Ngarzagamu

Biddefi

BAGIRMI

ETHIOPIA

ETHIOPIAN HIGHLANDS

Harer

Somali

gold,
ivory

Igala

Benue   pepper

GBO

Bonny

Old Calabar

BOBANGI

Ubangi

CONGO
BASIN

Congo

Babwa

Lomami

Lualaba

Nilotes

White Nile

Lake
Turkana

RIFT VALLEY

Galla

OROMO

Shebelli

Mogadishu

Baraawe

MPUMBU

TEKE

KUBA

RIFT VALLEY STATES

ivory

Lake
Victoria

Kikuyu

SULTANATE
OF ZANZIBAR

Pate
Lamu

Malindi

Mombasa

INDIAN
OCEAN

LOANGO
KAKONGO

Loango   NGOYO
Malembo

Cabinda

CONGO

Congo

Kwango

Ujiji

RIFT VALLEY

Lake
Tanganyika

Tabora

LUBA

Zanzibar

Indian traders

Brazil

Luanda
1574 to Portugal
Brazil

NDONGO

KASANJE

LUNDA

Kasai

Kwilu

MBUNDU

Benguela
1587 to Portugal
Brazil

OVIMBUNDU

Kilwa Kisiwani

Portuguese traders

Ovambo

Okavango

Cuando

Zambezi

Kafue

LOZI

Luangwa

Lake
Malawi

Ibo

MAKUA

gold,
ivory

Mozambique
1508 to Portugal

Vohemar

ginger

San

Herero

Shona

Tete
1532 to Portugal

Sena
1531 to Portugal

Khami
ROZWI

Sofala
1505 to Portugal

Quelimane
1544 to Portugal

Malagasy

Tananarive

Madagascar

Hova

Khoisan

Kalahari
Desert

Limpopo

Sotho

Xhosa

Vaal   Orange

Nguni

Inhambane

Delagoa Bay
1544 to Portugal,
1720–30 to Netherlands

Fort
Dauphin

Brazil

Cape Town
1652 to Netherlands

Cape of
Good Hope

CAPE COLONY

Sub-Saharan Africa

The arrival of Europeans in sub-Saharan Africa caused dislocations in old patterns of trade and cultural exchange. Nonetheless, outside influence was nowhere so extensive or systematic that it overwhelmed indigenous culture.

The geographical barriers of the oceans and the Sahara, and Africa's abundance of natural resources, had inhibited the growth of an African seafaring or long-distance trading culture. Even coastal trade was minimal until it was developed by the Portuguese and the Dutch. Nevertheless, the empires of the Sahel (the southern fringe of the Sahara), notably Songhai, traded gold, ivory, and slaves in exchange for salt, glass, and other luxuries. Other states traded with one another along the great river routes, especially in west Africa.

West Africa

Portuguese navigators first arrived in west Africa in the mid-15th century. The coastal bases they established drew trade away from the Upper Niger River. Following a long struggle with the Hausa people to the east, the Songhai empire was overthrown in 1591 by a Moroccan mercenary army, and a Moroccan governorship was established. Neither this nor the new African states on the Upper Niger—the Manding empire and the Bambara kingdoms of Segu and Kaarta—could match the power of Songhai.

South of the Sahara

The early 16th century saw the emergence of other states to the south of the Sahara, including the Mossi around Ouagadougou and, later, the Oyo states of the Niger delta. Asante and Dahomey emerged in the 17th century, first in the interior and later dominating the coast. By the late 18th century, both were centralized, bureaucratic kingdoms. South of the Equator was the Congo kingdom, where rivalry with Ndongo allowed

Mercenary

Describes hired foreign soldiers.

Curriculum Context

Describing the institutions and economies of African states such as Asante, Dahomey, Lunda, and Congo in the 16th to 18th centuries is a requirement of some world history curricula.

the Portuguese to establish a colony in Angola after 1575. Nevertheless, Ndongo's Queen Njinga (r.1624–63) prevented any further European expansion. Further inland, the powerful Lunda empire arose in the mid-18th century and pressed westward.

In the states of the southern edge of the Sahara, Islam made its greatest progress. From 1570, Idris Aloma of Kanem-Bornu created the most purely Islamic state in Africa and built up its power by importing firearms from the Ottomans and converting the Wadai and Bagirmi states to the east. An Islamic revival took place in Senegambia in the late 18th century.

East Africa

In east Africa, conflict arose between Islam and the Christian kingdom of Ethiopia. The conversion of the Funj to Islam was accompanied by a rebellion of Adal, an alliance of Islamic states, against Ethiopian rule in 1527. Ahmed Gran, an Adali imam, ravaged Ethiopia for 13 years. On the east African coast, Portugal established a string of bases to dominate Indian Ocean trade. At the end of the 17th century, the sultanate of Oman capitalized on a fierce conflict between the Portuguese and the Dutch by occupying most of the northern bases, and Omani and Indian trade across the Indian Ocean revived as a result.

Imam
A Muslim spiritual and political leader.

The slave trade

The most dramatic impact of Europeans on Africa was the transatlantic slave trade, which began early in the 16th century. A trade in slaves within Africa already existed, but the demand for labor in the plantations in the Americas and the willingness of many African states to deal with Europeans led to an explosion of the trade in the 17th century. States such as Dahomey waged war in their traditional manner to obtain slaves, or enslaved and sold parts of their own populations.

Curriculum Context

An important aspect of the slave trade is the role played by African governments, elites, merchants, and other groups in the sale of slaves to Europeans, as well as the impact of slavery on west and central Africa.

The Rise of Mughal India

In the 16th and 17th centuries, the Mughals created a vast and powerful empire across the Indian subcontinent.

KHANATE OF
KHIVA

Bukhara
Samarkand

Mery

Mashhad

HINDU K

to Persia & the Levant

SAFAVID
PERSIA

Herat

Balkh

to Safavid
Persia, 1588

Kandahar
1649, 1652

BALUCHISTAN

KIRTHAR RANGE

to Persia & Arabia

Arabian
Sea

(se

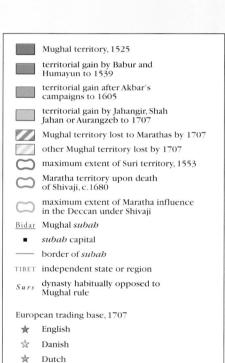

▨	Mughal territory, 1525
▨	territorial gain by Babur and Humayun to 1539
▨	territorial gain after Akbar's campaigns to 1605
▨	territorial gain by Jahangir, Shah Jahan or Aurangzeb to 1707
▨	Mughal territory lost to Marathas by 1707
▨	other Mughal territory lost by 1707
⬭	maximum extent of Suri territory, 1553
⬭	Maratha territory upon death of Shivaji, c.1680
⬭	maximum extent of Maratha influence in the Deccan under Shivaji
Bidar	Mughal *subah*
▪	*subah* capital
—	border of *subah*
TIBET	independent state or region
Surs	dynasty habitually opposed to Mughal rule

European trading base, 1707

★	English
☆	Danish
★	Dutch
★	French
☆	Portuguese
♨	Maratha raid, with date
⛩	mosque
—	trade route

Andijan

Kashgar
Yarkand
KHANATE OF KASHGAR

KHANATE OF
TURFAN

to Beijing

Khotan

KUNLUN MTS

Baltistan

Peshawar
Kashmir
(sub province)
Srinagar

Ladakh

TIBET

Lahore
Lahore

Lhasa

Multan
Delhi
1526, 1556
Panipat
Sikhs

HIMALAYAS

Gurkhas

Koch

recovered by
Ahoms, 1669

Nagas

Shans

TOUNGOU

Multan
Satnamis
Delhi
Sambhal

Kathmandu

Ahoms

Rathors
Rajputs
Jats
Desert
Fatehpur
Sikri
Agra

Oudh
Ayodhya
Surs

Jaipur
Ajmer

Ajmer
Ranthambhor
1569

Agra
Yamuna
Allahabad
Allahabad

Varanasi
Patna
Bihar
Bihar

Gaur

Cossimbazar
Baharampur

Bengal
Hooghly-
Chinsura

Dhaka

Chittagong

Jodhpur

Chittaurgarh
Udaipur 1568

Sisodiyas

Sironj
1703

Bundelas

Chandannagar
Calcutta

ARAKAN

to southeast Asia, China & Japan

Malwa
Ujjain
1703

Ahmadabad

Mandu
Asirgarh
1601

Narmada

Mandla

Gondwana

Baleshwar

Bay of
Bengal

Vadodara
1706
Bharuch
1685
Champanir

Gawilgarh

Cuttack

Surat
1664
Diu
Daman

Khandesh

Burhanpur
1670
Karanja
1670

Imad Shahis

Orissa

Pipli

Irrawaddy

Nizam
Shahis
Ahmadnagar

Aurangabad
1685
DECCAN
Berar

Vasai
Bombay
Chaul

Ahmadnagar
1657

Qutb Shahis

Bidar

Golconda
1687
Golconda

Bimlipatam
Vishakhapatnam

Kakinada

Palakollu

Bijapur
Bijapur
1666
Krishna

Bidar
1686,

Machilipatnam

Vengurla
Goa

Adil Shahis

Hubli
1673

Koppal
1677

Aravidus

to southeast Asia

Anjidiv
Island
Karwar

Vijayanagara

Chitradurga
1695
Sira

Coondapoor

Pulicat
Madras

Mangalore

Bangalore

Vellore
1677
Arani
1677
Sadras

Cannanore
Tellicherry
Calicut

Mysore

to Udaiyars,
1672
Gingee

Pondicherry
Fort St David
Porto Novo
Tranquebar
Nagappattinam

Cranganur
Cochin
Porakad
Kayankulam
Quilon
Anjengo

Pallipuram
Madurai

MYSORE
Udaiyars

Kaveri
Tanjore
1677

MALABAR COAST

MADURAI

Jaffna

Mannar
Tuticorin
Kayalpatnam

Trincomalee

Puttalam

Batticaloa

Manapadu
Negombo
Colombo

Sautus

Ceylon

Galle
Matara

to southeast Asia

The Rise of Mughal India

The eastward migration of Mongols and Tatars in the late 15th and early 16th centuries meant that the Mughals, a people descended from Timur's Mongols, were driven out of the principality they had established in Ferghana. Under their leader Babur (r.1501–30), the Mughals conquered an area around Kabul in 1504 and made the first of several exploratory invasions of India in 1519, culminating in a full-scale attempt in 1526.

The Indian subcontinent was a patchwork of Muslim and Hindu states; the Rajput lands southwest of Delhi, the southern Hindu kingdom of Vijayanagara, and the Afghan Lodi sultanate of Delhi were the most powerful.

Artillery

The section of an army that uses heavy weaponry, such as cannons and rockets.

Mughal conquests

Babur's force of 12,000 men, supported by artillery, overcame the army of Ibrahim Shah Lodi at Panipat in 1526. By Babur's death, the former Lodi lands had been subdued, while his son Humayun (r.1530–40; 1555–56) invaded Gujarat in 1535. In the 1540s, however, a rebellion of the Afghan Sur dynasty of south Bihar captured the Gangetic plain and Delhi, forcing Humayun to take refuge in Persia. Only in 1555 did Humayun succeed in reoccupying Delhi.

Babur's grandson Akbar (r.1556–1605) regained the lands lost to the Surs. In 1572, his conquest of Gujarat brought access to the sea, while control of Bengal in 1576 secured India's richest region. By 1605, Mughal advance into the Deccan had begun with the subjugation of Khandesh and Berar; the loyalty of the Rajputs was assured by military force and dynastic intermarriage. Akbar's reign brought administrative efficiency and social reform. The empire was divided into provinces administered by professional civil servants appointed on merit. The sophisticated Akbar promoted religious toleration throughout his empire.

Curriculum Context

How the Mughals were able to conquer India is fundamental to understanding their success at uniting the peoples of the subcontinent.

Trade with Europeans

A number of external powers also arrived in India after 1500. The Portuguese acquired trading bases at Goa, Daman, and Diu in the early 16th century. In general, the Indians found mercantile benefits in cooperating with Europeans. By 1500, Indian banking and credit facilities supported a commercial network that covered most of Asia and east Africa, and extended as far as Moscow. Since Roman times, Europeans had exchanged silver or gold for Indian silks, cottons, spices, and dyes, and European access to the silver mines of Latin America made possible a huge increase in this trade. Trading links with European companies became more and more important in the Mughal economy.

Agriculture and industry

Mughal agriculture was highly efficient and cash crops (indigo, cotton, sugar, opium, pepper, and later tobacco) were developed within a centrally controlled internal market. Indian industry, based on cheap labor and proven, low-level technology, included both the world's largest textile industry, with products exported worldwide, and an iron industry producing high-quality steel and cannon to equal any in Europe.

Mughal decline

The Mughals kept a standing army of about one million men who were equipped with weapons that, until the 18th century, rivaled European arms. Yet the vast Mughal empire was already fragmenting by the death of the last great emperor, Aurangzeb (r.1658–1707). Religious intolerance had grown under Akbar's successors—Jahangir, Shah Jahan, and Aurangzeb—leading to increasingly frequent revolts, even as the empire reached its greatest territorial extent with the conquest of Ahmadnagar (1636), Bijapur (1686), and Golconda (1687). As bases of the Dutch and British East India companies spread in the later 17th century, largely displacing the Portuguese, the Hindu Marathas of the Western Ghats were already asserting their independence from the Mughal empire.

Curriculum Context

It may be revealing for students to compare Akbar's method of government and his religious ideas with those of the other Mughal emperors.

The Successors to Mughal India

In the 18th century, Mughal power declined as Maratha power increased, but all of India faced threats from French and British expansion.

KHANATE OF BUKHARA

Amu Darya

Balkh.
Balkh

HINDU

.Herat

Abdalis

Helmand

PERSIA

AFGHANISTAN

Kandahar.

Ghilzais

Seistan

KIRTHAR RANGE

Kalat

Ahmadzais
Makran

That

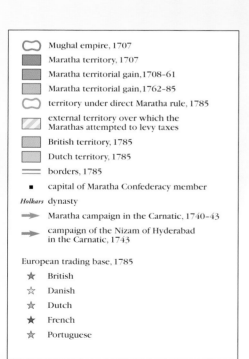

Mughal empire, 1707

Maratha territory, 1707

Maratha territorial gain, 1708–61

Maratha territorial gain, 1762–85

territory under direct Maratha rule, 1785

external territory over which the Marathas attempted to levy taxes

British territory, 1785

Dutch territory, 1785

borders, 1785

■ capital of Maratha Confederacy member

Holkars dynasty

➤ Maratha campaign in the Carnatic, 1740–43

➤ campaign of the Nizam of Hyderabad in the Carnatic, 1743

European trading base, 1785

★ British

☆ Danish

★ Dutch

★ French

☆ Portuguese

Kashgar
Yarkand
Khotan
Baltistan
Swat
Srinagar
Kashmir
LADAKH
Indus
LAHORE
Lahore
PUNJAB
Sikhs
Multan
Chenab
HIMALAYAS
Brahmaputra
Bhutan
ASSAM
Nagas
Shans
Sutlej
Karnal
1739
Panipat
1761
DELHI
ROHIL-
KHAND
Delhi
1757
Rampur
NEPAL
Gurkhas
Kathmandu
BURMA
Chins
Jats
Farrukhabad
Ayodhya
BENGAL
Dhaka
AGRA
Agra
Yamuna
OUDH
Ganges
Allahabad
Ghazipur
Patna
Bihar
Cossimbazar
Baharampur
Chittagong
ARAKAN
Irrawaddy
Rajputs
Ganges
Benares
(Varanasi)
Buxar
1764
BIHAR
Plassey
1757
Hooghly-
Chinsura
Jaipur
Ajmer
Allahabad
Bundelkhand
Chandannagar
1757
Calcutta
1756
Jaisalmer
Thar Desert
RAJPUTANA
Jodhpur
Sindhias
Sironj
Sambalpur
Baleshwar
Udaipur
Malwa
Bhopal
Orissa
Ujjain
Narmada
Mahanadi
Cuttack
Gaikwars
Ahmadabad
Mandu
Maheshwar
Khandesh
Burhanpur
Bhonsles
Pipli
Gujarat
Khambhat
Baroda
Bharuch
Songarh
Nagpur
Berar
Diu
Surat
Holkars
Chandrapur
Daman
Vasai
Ahmadnagar
DECCAN
Bombay
Poona
Peshwars
Udgir
1760
The Nizam
Bimlipatam
Vishakhapatnam
Chaul
WESTERN
Satara
Konkan
Bijapur
GOLCONDA
Hyderabad
Yanam
Kolhapur
Bijapur
Krishna
Narasapur
Palakollu
Machilipatnam
Nizampatam
Vengurla
lost 1780
lost 1776
Gooty
NORTHERN CIRCARS
GOA
Goa
Karwar
MYSORE
Anjidiv Island
Honavar
Damalcherry
1740
Pulicat
WESTERN GHATS
CARNATIC
Coondapoor
lost 1776
Ambur
1760
Arcot
1751
Madras
Sadras
Mangalore
Wandiwash
1760
Pondicherry
1748
Mysore
Kaveri
Fort St David
1746, 1758
Cannanore
Tellicherry
Mahé
MALABAR
Porto
Novo
Tranquebar
Karikal
Nagappattinam
Calicut
Chetwal
Trichinopoly
1741, 1752
Tanjore
Cranganur
COCHIN
Pallipuram
Madurai
Jaffna
Cochin
Mannar
Trincomalee
Porakad
TRAVANCORE
Kayankulam
Tuticorin
Batticaloa
Quilon
Kayalpatnam
Puttalam
Kandy
Anjengo
Manapadu
Negombo
KANDY
Colombo
Ceylon
Galle
Matara

The Successors to Mughal India

The beginning of the decline of Mughal power in India is variously dated to 1707 (death of Aurangzeb), 1739 (sack of Delhi by the Persians), 1757 (victory of Robert Clive at Plassey), or even 1761 (defeat of the Marathas by the Afghans at Panipat).

By the last quarter of the 18th century, India had suffered a long period of devastating wars and foreign intervention, and the major powers in the subcontinent were the Maratha Confederacy, Mysore, and the British East India Company.

Reasons for Mughal decline

The empire had reached its natural frontiers in Assam, Nepal, and the far south of India. With no fresh lands to dispense, the emperor could not keep the loyalty of the class of public officials, or *mansabdars*, without high taxation. The mansabdars became directly involved in trade themselves and sought ways of making their wealth hereditary rather than reverting to the emperor at their death. Provincial governors and viceroys (subadars and nabobs) became increasingly independent in the 18th century.

Curriculum Context

In some states, students are asked to explain why the Mughal Empire declined and regional powers such as the Marathas became powerful.

Rise of the Marathas

The greatest threat to the Mughal empire came from the Marathas, a Hindu people from the Western Ghats. Under Sivaji (r.1647–80), they began to raid extensively across central India, sacking Surat, the empire's main port, in 1664. Support from Hindu merchants enabled the Marathas to acquire superior weaponry, which, combined with great mobility, made them formidable opponents. Mughal military problems multiplied in the 18th century. In 1739, the Persian leader Nadir Shah (r.1736–47) defeated a Mughal army at Karnal and sacked Delhi. In 1740, the Marathas invaded the Carnatic; their defeat of the nabob at Damalcherry prompted intervention by the semi-independent nizam (ruler) of Hyderabad.

French and British intervention

By 1744, both French and British East India companies had been drawn into the conflict. In 1746, the French occupied Madras, the principal British base in the Carnatic. The French and their protégé Chanda Sahib deposed the nizam's appointed nabob of Arcot in 1749. The nizam was killed, and his successor appointed a French administrator Joseph Dupleix governor of Mughal south India in return for a military alliance. The British Company allied itself with Mysore and the Marathas, and Robert Clive won a spectacular victory over Chanda Sahib and the French at Arcot. While Maratha forces overran the west of the nizam's territories, Clive forced the French to surrender at Trichinopoly in 1752. In 1756, an independent Mughal nawab in Bengal, Siraj ud-Daulah (r.1756–57), captured the British Company's base at Calcutta. Clive responded by securing the loyalty of the Bengali army commander and using the Company's ships to transport troops to Bengal from the Carnatic. The defeat of Siraj at Plassey led to the first major British territorial acquisition in India. In the Carnatic, hostilities in 1758 led to the British capture of Pondicherry in 1761 and the end of French power in India.

Protégé

Someone who is protected and trained.

Maratha decline and British dominance

The Marathas raided widely in the north and east, prompting the Muslim rulers of Rohilkhand to seek an alliance with Ahmad Shah Durrani (r.1747–73) of Afghanistan. In 1761 at Panipat, a large, well-equipped Maratha army was routed by the Afghans, ending any chance that the Marathas might reconstitute the Mughal empire. Ahmad Shah's army withdrew after sacking Delhi, leaving the British East India Company uniquely placed to benefit. In the following two decades, the territorial foundations of British rule in India were laid: Bengal and Bihar (1765), the Northern Circars (1768), and the cities of Benares and Ghazipur (1775) passed into British Company hands.

Curriculum Context

The impact of British and French commercial and military initiatives on politics, economy, and society in India is an example of the expanding global influence of European economic power.

Ming China

Ming China was a prosperous empire whose government limited external trade, but it declined and fell to the Manchus in 1644.

DZUNGARIA

Kalmyk Tatars

Turfan · Hami

Anxi

Suzhou ·
Ganzhou ·
Liangzhou ·
Ningxia

QILIAN MTS

Lake Qinghai
Xining ·
Lanzhou

QIN MTS

Chamdo ·

Chengdu

Chongc

Luzhou ·

Zhaotong

Dali ·
Menghua ·
Yunnan ·
Yunnan

Nago Hills

Mekong
Jinsha
Yalong

YU
(AN

borders, c.1590

Ming territory, c.1590

Ming tributary or buffer state, c.1590

area subject to attack by Japanese *Wako* pirates in the 15th and 16th centuries

area occupied by *Wako* pirates after 1550

Wako pirate base area

popular uprisings, 1636–41

kingdom of Zhang Xianzhong, 1641–44

kingdom of Li Zucheng, 1641–45

Chinese trade route under the Ming empire

Portuguese trade route

Spanish "Manila Galleon" trade route

★ Chinese trading base

☆ Dutch trading base

☆ Portuguese trading base

★ Spanish trading base

silk   major export from China

silver   major import to China

Ming national capital, with date

■ Ming provincial capital

Great Wall

Willow Palisade

canal of the Ming period

modern coastline and drainage where altered

migration of Mongol and Tatar nomads, 16th century

Mongols

Jürchen
(Manchus)

Kaiyuan
Shenyang
(Mukden)

Liaoyang

Haizhou

Liaodong

Rehe

Shanhaiguan

Kalgan

Jinzhou

Datong

Beijing
1421 onwards

Sanggan

Taiyuan

Zhili

Wonsan

*Sea of
Japan*

Pyongyang

Dengzhou

Seoul

CHAOXIAN
(KOREA)

Shanxi

Fen

Pingdu

Ji'nan

Ulsan

Pusan

RIBEN
(JAPAN)

Osaka

Da Yunhe (Grand Canal)

present course of Yellow river

Shandong

*Yellow
Sea*

Kaifeng

Yellow river
1324–1853

Lake
Hongze

Huai'an

Henan

Huai

Nagasaki

Han

Nanjing
1368–1403

*copper, silver,
spices*

Nanzhili

cotton textiles,
silk, wine

Wushan

Wuchang

Jingzhou

Hangzhou

Mingzhou
(Ningbo)

*East
China
Sea*

Jujiang

Lake
Pengli

Zhejiang

Yangtze

Huguang

Lake
Dongting

Nanchang

Wenzhou

Tanzhou

Jiangxi

Yuanling

Haobaijiang
(Naha)

Hengzhou

Fuzhou

Fujian

Ganzhou

Tingzhou

Jilong

Zhangzhou

Xiamen
(Amoy)

*Taiwan
(Formosa)*

Guilin

Tainan

Fort Zeelandia

Guangdong

Xi

Guangzhou
(Canton)

cotton textiles,
ironware, silk, tea

Macao

cotton textiles,
porcelain, silk

Qiongzhou

*South
China
Sea*

Dajiang
(Port San Vicente)

Hainan

to Champa and Siam

from Goa

to the Indonesian archipelago

Pengjiashilan
(Pangasinan)

*Philippine
Islands*

to Central America

Lusong
(Manila)

*silver
from Europe*

*silver
from Central
America*

*from
Central America*

Ming China

By the beginning of the 16th century, the great Ming imperial dynasty of China was on the decline. The Ming reconquest of the country from the Mongols had been followed by the long process of rebuilding China's economy and by a period of aggressive foreign policy.

Repeated invasions of Mongolia ended in 1449 with the capture of the Mongol emperor and the adoption of a new defensive strategy. In the same period, extensive maritime expeditions of admiral Zheng He spread Ming military and economic power as far as the east coast of Africa, but they ended with the admiral's death in 1433. An indication of Ming China's changing priorities was the transfer in 1421 of the capital from Nanjing in the heart of the maritime trading region to Beijing near the Mongol border. Any prospect of Chinese maritime contact with Europe vanished.

The Ming economy

Ming economic policy favored a regulated and self-sufficient domestic economy. Peace and stability after 1449 brought a steady population increase, and a huge manufacturing and trading economy emerged. Long-distance trade prospered, despite government attempts at regulation and despite the monopolies operated by regional merchant oligarchies. Cotton fields in northern China supplied a booming textile industry. Along with other commodities (such as silk and tea), cotton goods were exported to Japan in exchange for metals and spices, and to southeast Asia in exchange for silver from the Americas. The Portuguese established a permanent trading base at Macao in 1557, and the Dutch built a fortified settlement on Taiwan (Formosa) in 1622. Relations between these European merchants and the Ming authorities were frequently uncomfortable.

Ming China under attack

One consequence of efforts to control export and import was the growth of the *wako* in the mid-16th century. These pirate-trader bands were mainly based in southern Japan, from where they descended on the Chinese coast from the 1520s onward, until the spread of Japanese central authority deprived them of their bases. Their raids coincided with two invasions of northern China by Mongol forces under Altan Khan (r.1543–83), which were only repelled at great cost.

In 1592, the Ming vassal state of Korea was attacked by a Japanese army of 200,000 troops equipped with firearms. The Ming responded by deploying an army said to have numbered one million men and a substantial naval force. The Japanese were driven back to the south coast of Korea after heavy fighting; a second invasion in 1597–98 met with the same fate.

End of the Ming dynasty

Plagues and crop failures caused devastation in much of the north of the country at the end of the 16th century, and growing corruption in the imperial bureaucracy fueled popular resentment. Harsh tax raises on agriculture and requisitions for the war effort provoked open insurrection in cities throughout China and widespread peasant revolts after 1627. Ming authority crumbled: Liaodong and territories north of the Wall were annexed by a new rival power, the Manchus, who also engineered a successful coup against the Ming-allied rulers of Korea. After 1641, rebel regimes sprang up in north and west China proper, led by Li Zucheng and Zhang Xianzhong. The last Ming emperor committed suicide as Li's forces entered Beijing in 1644. The Manchus under Dorgun (r.1628–50) had laid claim to the leadership of China in 1636. Responding to a request for aid by the Ming, they drove Li Zucheng from Beijing in 1644 and then proceeded to install their own Qing dynasty.

Bureaucracy

A government with fixed rules, specialized functions, and a clear hierarchy of authority.

Curriculum Context

Some curricula ask students to explain how the Manchus overthrew the Ming dynasty.

The Rise of Manchu China

The Manchu Chinese empire was founded in 1644 and remained powerful until the end of the 18th century.

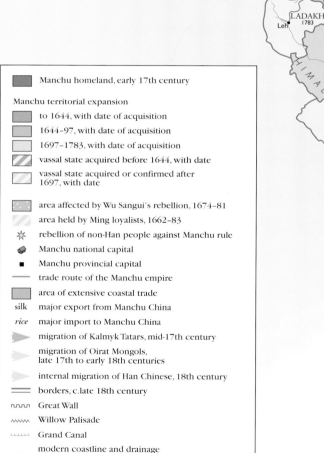

Semipalatinsk

Lake Balkhash

Dzungars ✸ 1765   Oirat Mongols 1750–57 ✸

Ili Protectorate 1755–57

Ili •

Isyk Kul   **Dzungars**

DZUNGARIA

territory added to Gansu 1759

Urumqi •

TIEN SHAN

Turfan •

KASHGARIA 1759   Aksu ✸ Muslims ✸ 1758–59

Kashgar •
gems, silk, tea to Middle East

Yarkand •

Xinjiang 1724–60

EASTERN TURKESTAN

KUNLUN MTS

Khotan •
gems, silk, tea to Middle East

LADAKH 1783
Leh •

HIMALAYAS

Xizang 1718–20

TIBET

Lhasa •

Tashilumpo •
NEPAL 1792   SIKKIM

Darjeeling •   BHUTAN 1730

Brahmaputra
Ahoms

	Manchu homeland, early 17th century

Manchu territorial expansion

	to 1644, with date of acquisition
	1644–97, with date of acquisition
	1697–1783, with date of acquisition
	vassal state acquired before 1644, with date
	vassal state acquired or confirmed after 1697, with date
✸	area affected by Wu Sangui's rebellion, 1674–81
	area held by Ming loyalists, 1662–83
✸	rebellion of non-Han people against Manchu rule
	Manchu national capital
■	Manchu provincial capital
—	trade route of the Manchu empire
	area of extensive coastal trade
silk	major export from Manchu China
rice	major import to Manchu China
	migration of Kalmyk Tatars, mid-17th century
	migration of Oirat Mongols, late 17th to early 18th centuries
	internal migration of Han Chinese, 18th century
=	borders, c.late 18th century
⌐⌐⌐	Great Wall
⌒⌒⌒	Willow Palisade
⌐⌐⌐	Grand Canal
	modern coastline and drainage where altered

RUSSIAN EMPIRE

Lake Baykal

Irkutsk

Chita

Nerchinsk

furs, gold, silver from Russia

Kyakhta

cotton fabrics, silk, tea to Russia

Uliastay

Khalka 1697

1696

Ulan Bator

Inner Mongolian Plateau

Setsen

OUTER MONGOLIA

Tushiyetu

Gobi Desert

Chahar 1635

INNER MONGOLIA

Dolonnur

Kalgan

Rehe

zhou

Ganzhou

Alashan Eleuth

Ordos Desert

Ningxia

Yellow

Beijing

Zhili 1644

Muslims 1781–84

Lake Qinghai

Hui Muslims 1781–84

Lanzhou

Gansu 1649

Taiyuan 1644

Shanxi 1644–45

Shandong 1645

Ji'nan

Huai'an

Shaanxi 1645–46

Xi'an (Chang'an)

Yellow river 1324–1853

Henan 1645

Kaifeng

Han

DABA MTS

Jin Chuans 1746–49

Sichuan 1646

Wushan

Hubei 1645

Wuchang

Anhui 1645

Hefei

Nanjing

Jiangsu 1645

Chengdu

Chongqing

Yalong

Lake Dongting

Tanzhou

Nanchang

Wenzhou

Zhejiang 1646

tribal risings 1726–29

Guizhou 1658

Hunan 1647–50

Jiangxi 1649–52

Fuzhou

Dali

Guiyang

Guilin (Guizhou)

Yunnan 1659

Yunnan

Yao 1790

Guangdong 1650–55

Ganzhou

Fujian 1646

Xiamen (Amoy)

aboriginal rising 1787–88

Fort Zeelandia

Guangxi 1650–52

Xi

Guangzhou (Canton)

Macao

cotton fabrics, ironware, porcelain, silk to southeast Asia

porcelain, silk, tea to Europe

YUENAN (ANNAM) 1666

South China Sea

Qiongzhou

Hainan

opium, silver from India

raw cotton, rice, woods from southeast Asia

IENLO SIAM)

LAOS

Amur 1689 (to Russia 1650–89)

Heje Kiakia

Aigun

Solon

Albazin (Yakesa)

Mergen

Heilungjiang

Qiqihar

MANCHURIA

ginseng, soya beans from Manchuria

Kurka

Jilin

Jürchen (Manchus)

Hunchun

Shenyang (Mukden)

Khorchin 1629–30

Niuzhuang

Liaodong

Jinzhou

Wonsan

CHAOXIAN (KOREA) 1637

Seoul

Sea of Japan

RIBEN (JAPAN)

Kyoto

present course of Yellow river

Dengzhou

Pusan

cotton fabrics, tea to Manchuria

Yellow Sea

Nagasaki

copper from Japan

medicines, silk, sugar to Japan

Huai

Hangzhou

Mingzhou

East China Sea

Lake Pengli

Taiwan (Formosa) 1683

The Rise of Manchu China

The Manchus originated as one of the Jürchen tribes—themselves part of a larger group of Tungusic (Siberian) peoples—from the area to the north of the Korean peninsula adjoining the Han Chinese enclave of Liaodong.

They began to emerge as a political force under the leadership of Nurhachi (r.1586–1626), who imposed a Mongol-style military administration in 1615.

The Manchus take control

In the 1620s and 1630s, the peoples united by Nurhachi profited from Ming weakness to establish control over Mongol lands just north of the Wall, the Liaodong basin, and the Ming vassal state of Korea. Nurhachi's son Dorgun (r.1628–50) gained control of Beijing in 1644 and acted as regent to his nephew, who was installed as the first Manchu (Qing) emperor of China. Over the next 15 years, Ming resistance was suppressed, with the far southwestern province of Yunnan the last to fall.

The Manchus adopted a subtle approach to administrative reform. Manchu officials were given senior posts in existing Ming institutions, and military garrisons were set up in the major provincial cities, but new structures were not imposed wholesale. The Manchus were initially quick to require cultural changes, but their numerical inferiority to the Han Chinese meant that, by the 18th century, their culture had become fully assimilated. Their most significant contribution was to inject an unprecedented dynamism and efficiency into Chinese political and military life.

Resistance to Manchu rule

In 1674, an attempt by the Beijing government to assert its authority over the southern province of

Regent

Someone who governs a state when the sovereign is absent, or too young or disabled to rule.

Guangdong, which had been allowed considerable autonomy, prompted a popular revolt led by Wu Sangui, governor of Yunnan and Guizhou. Wu, supported by Shang Zhixin of Guangdong and Geng Jingzhong of Fujian, was only defeated after five years of campaigning. At the same time, the government was confronted with a rebellion by the Ming-loyalist warlord Zheng Jing. After this, only the uprising of non-Han tribal peoples in Yunnan in 1726–29 disrupted more than a century of internal peace and stability for Manchu China.

Expansion of the Manchu empire

A campaign of territorial expansion resulted in the creation of a great Eurasian land empire. Russian incursions into the Amur region ended in 1689. The Manchus then subdued the formidable Dzungars (West Mongols) and, by 1783, Manchu colonial administration had been extended to Tibet and its vassal states (Bhutan, Sikkim, and Ladakh) and the former Turkic khanates of eastern Turkestan. Burma and Laos were reduced to vassal status, and Manchu troops were poised to invade Nepal and Annam.

Peace and prosperity

Peace and prosperity caused a demographic explosion within the Manchu empire. The Chinese population swelled from 100 million in 1650 to 300 million in 1800. This expansion created growing tensions. A ban imposed by the Manchus on the settlement of Han Chinese north of the Wall led to largescale internal migrations in the late 17th and 18th centuries from the overpopulated Yangtze basin and southeast to new agricultural lands in the west and southwest. The authorities maintained Chinese external trade but were able to restrict foreign merchants to Guangzhou in the south and Kyakhta in the north. The export of Chinese luxury goods for silver continued to ensure a strong monetary economy.

> **Curriculum Context**
>
> The Manchus doubled the size of the Chinese empire, thereby creating a multiethnic society and changing the shape of China.

> **Curriculum Context**
>
> An important aspect of European trade with China is the ability of the Chinese government to control it.

Japan and the Shogunate

The 16th to 18th centuries in Japan were a time of productivity, prosperity, and increasingly centralized government.

MING CHINESE EMPIRE

Korea Bay

Pyongyang 1592

Wonsan

Kaesong 1592

Seoul 1592

Imjin

KOREA

Nakdong

Yellow Sea

Ulsa

Tongnae

Pusan

Mokpo

Sunchon

Tsushima

Fuchu

Nag

Hirado

to China, Indo-China and Siam

Nagasa

Goto Islands

Shimaba (Hara cas 1637–

to Taiwan and Indonesia

An

Oda land, 1560

area conquered by Nobunaga and Hideyoshi by 1582

main *daimyo* house opposed to Hideyoshi, 1582

Mori   *daimyo* house, 16th–17th centuries

campaigns of Hideyoshi, 1584–90

Hideyoshi's first invasion of Korea, 1592

Hideyoshi's second invasion of Korea, 1597–98

Korean and Ming Chinese counteroffensives

main areas of Korean resistance to Hideyoshi

Japanese base in Korea retained after 1593

Hideyoshi victory

castle town

Japanese peasant revolt against Hideyoshi's land survey

victory of Tokugawa Ieyasu or his successors

area with significant number of Christian converts

Hirado   trading port used by Europeans

"Five Highways" of Tokugawa Japan

coastal shipping route

Sea of Japan

Hokkaido

- Hakodate
- Miyuma
- Hirosaki
- Hachinohe
- Noshiro
- Akita
- Morioka
- Miyako
- Senpoku
- Honjo
- Shinjo
- Ichinoseki
- Shonai
- Ozaki
- Tsuruoka
- Sendai
- Yamagata
- Sado
- Tsukahara
- Niigata
- Shibata
- Yonezawa
- Fukushima
- Wajima
- Nagaoka
- Aizu
- Iwaki
- Takata
- Shirakawa

JAPAN

Uesugi

- Nikko
- Toyama
- Zenkoji
- Utsunomiya
- Kanazawa
- Sasa
- Takeda
- Takasaki
- Maeda
- Shibata
- Hojo
- Oki
- Honshu
- Fukui
- Edo
- Choshi
- Obama
- Sekigahara 1600
- Iida
- Odawara 1590
- 1590
- Matsue
- Tottori
- Nagoya
- Numazu
- Yonago
- Fukuchiyama
- Akechi
- Tokugawa
- Shimoda
- Ukita
- Kyoto
- Azuchi
- Yoshida
- Hamada
- Himeji
- Momoyama
- Ise
- Mori
- Okayama
- Kobe
- Osaka 1614-15
- Toba
- Hiroshima
- Sakai
- Hagi
- Takamatsu
- 1584-85
- Shimonoseki
- Imabari
- Tokushima
- Kitakyushu
- Matsuyama
- Tanabe
- Shingu
- Funai
- Chosokabe
- Kochi
- Oshima
- Sagaseki
- Shikoku
- Uwajima
- Higo
- Otomo
- Nobeoka
- Yashiro
- Umekita
- Kyushu
- Shimazu
- Miyazaki
- Kagoshima
- Yamagawa
- Tanegashima

westward coastal route
eastward coastal route
Nakasendo
Koshu Kaido
Tokaido
Nikko Kaido
Oshu Kaido
Osaka–Edo route
1587
1584-85

PACIFIC OCEAN

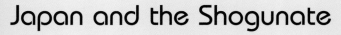

Japan and the Shogunate

The last century of the Ashikaga shogunate (1338–1573) in Japan was dominated by the political fragmentation arising from the Onin war of 1467–77. Following this protracted civil conflict, real power devolved to small, feudal units subject to the changing allegiances of local lords (daimyo). The authority of the emperor and his military commander, the shogun, was only nominal.

Instability was heightened by ever more frequent popular uprisings, often incited by the powerful Buddhist monasteries.

Noh drama

Japanese drama on a heroic theme with very stylized dancing, action, costumes, and scenery.

Economy and culture

Japanese trade and industry grew steadily in the later 15th and early 16th centuries. Japan also remained culturally vibrant. Many daimyo patronized such art forms as noh drama, poetry, and painting; traveling balladeers and dancers created a popular culture.

Clan

A group of people with a common ancestor.

Nobunaga and Hideyoshi

In 1568, Nobunaga, lord of the Oda clan, captured the imperial capital Kyoto and embarked on the destruction of Buddhist temples and slaughter of the monks. He also constructed an entirely new type of castle at Azuchi. In contrast to earlier mountain strongholds, Azuchi was built to dominate the rice fields and communications of the plain and was an administrative center as well as a fortress.

Under the leadership of Nobunaga's lieutenant Hideyoshi, Oda forces overran the lands of their rivals in central Japan then expanded eastward. After Nobunaga's death in 1582, Hideyoshi became ruler of most of central Japan in alliance with Tokugawa Ieyasu, his greatest rival. In 1590, Hideyoshi's capture of the Hojo clan's castle at Odawara also gave him control of eastern Japan.

Hideyoshi introduced political changes to prevent further unrest. He disarmed the peasantry and insisted that the samurai (warrior-class) live in castle towns, so that potentially rebellious farming communities could no longer rely on local samurai support. Taxation was reformed, which initially caused widespread unrest. Trade was brought under government control, and Christianity, which had spread from the Portuguese base at Nagasaki (founded 1572), was suppressed. Ieyasu succeeded Hideyoshi and continued his policies, as did subsequent shoguns of the Tokugawa dynasty, which he founded in 1603.

Curriculum Context

Studies of Japan's relationship with Europeans between the 16th and 18th centuries may focus on the consequences of its policy of limiting contact with foreigners.

Persecution and repression

Christianity, persecuted under Hidetada (r.1605–23), was eradicated by the massacre of 37,000 Japanese Christians at Hara castle (1638). Social and economic stability was maintained by strict segregation of farming and trade, a ban on private investment, and official discouragement of any contact between different parts of the country that did not use the closely controlled Five Highways. Portuguese ships were banned from Japan in 1639, export restricted to Dutch and Chinese bases at Nagasaki, and Japanese citizens were forbidden to travel abroad (while those long resident in ports throughout Asia were forbidden to return). The construction of large ships was banned in 1638 to prevent the Japanese from traveling abroad.

Unrest and opposition

The17th and 18th centuries were remarkable for economic prosperity, agricultural productivity, booming cities, and technological advancement, but economic and social ills began to accumulate. By the mid-18th century, many peasants had left the land. Famine, natural disasters, and government corruption provoked frequent peasant uprisings after 1760. The late 18th century saw the growth of an opposition movement around the emperor to the rule of the Tokugawa shoguns and a new awareness of the threat from expanding European influence in Asia.

Curriculum Context

In some states, students are asked to explain the character of centralized feudalism in Japan under the Tokugawa shogunate and the reasons for Japan's political stability and economic growth.

Southeast Asia

Between 1500 and 1800, mainland states rose and fell, while island states felt the influence of European and Islamic traders.

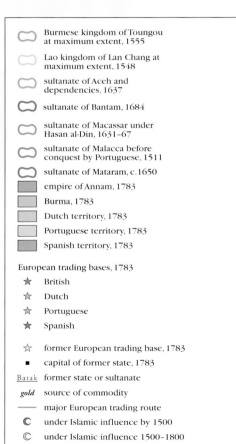

Burmese kingdom of Toungou at maximum extent, 1555

Lao kingdom of Lan Chang at maximum extent, 1548

sultanate of Aceh and dependencies, 1637

sultanate of Bantam, 1684

sultanate of Macassar under Hasan al-Din, 1631–67

sultanate of Malacca before conquest by Portuguese, 1511

sultanate of Mataram, c.1650

empire of Annam, 1783

Burma, 1783

Dutch territory, 1783

Portuguese territory, 1783

Spanish territory, 1783

European trading bases, 1783

★ British

☆ Dutch

☆ Portuguese

★ Spanish

☆ former European trading base, 1783

■ capital of former state, 1783

Batak former state or sultanate

gold source of commodity

— major European trading route

☾ under Islamic influence by 1500

☾ under Islamic influence 1500–1800

EMPIRE/
EMPIRE

Zhangzhou

Guangzhou
(Canton)

Macao

Hoa

Hainan

Hue
Hoi An
(Fai Po)

COCHIN-
CHINA

Vijaya
(Qui Nhon)

Champa

South China Sea

to Japan

Fort San Salvador
(Jilong)

Fort Zeelandia

Taiwan
(Formosa)
1624 to Dutch,
1683 to Manchu empire

to Acapulco

gold

Luzon

Manila

gold

Mindoro

gold

Philippine Islands

Samar

Panay

gold

Cebu

Leyte

Philippine
Sea

Palawan

Negros

gold

Mindanao

Balambangan

MAGINDANAO

gold

Zamboanga

gold

Sulu Archipelago

gold

Brunei

gold

Celebes Sea

Halmahera

Manado

Ternate

Tidore

Sambas

Borneo

gold

gold

Sukadana

gold

Belitung

Sula Islands

gold

Celebes

gold

Moluccas

Ceram

Amboina

Buru

Banda

Kai
Islands

Banjarmasin

Macassar

Banda Sea

Aru
Islands

Java Sea

Japara
Demak

Batavia
Cirebon

Rembang

Tegal

Java

Gresik
Surabaya

Yogyakarta

gold

pepper

Bali

Lombok

Bima

gold

gold

Flores

Sumbawa

Sumba

Alore

Solor

Wetar

Tanimbar
Islands

Timor

Kupang

Timor Sea

Southeast Asia

European influence grew in the islands of southeast Asia between 1500 and 1800, yet the vitality of the states and peoples of the mainland restricted foreign incursions to a minimum. The trading economies of the island-states of the Indonesian archipelago rivaled those of the European powers until the mid-18th century.

On the mainland, the Burmese, Arakanese, Thai, Khmer, Vietnamese, and Laotian peoples all established or consolidated existing states between 1500 and 1800.

Burmese empire building

Toungou, led by Tabin Shweti (r.1535–50), expanded north to incorporate the ancient Burmese capital of Pagan and south to overrun the Mon kingdom of Pegu. Laotians from Lan Chang extended their control westward over the Thai state of Chiangmai in 1548. Toungou annexed Ava and wrested Chiangmai from the Laotians in 1556. This Burmese empire survived until 1600, when a new Burmese state, based on Ava, emerged to dominate much the same area.

Vietnamese states

The Vietnamese state of Annam steadily expanded southward at the expense of the Hindu kingdom of Champa, capturing its capital Vijaya in 1471. Once Vietnamese began to populate the central coast, they proved hard for Hanoi to control. The kingdom split around 1600: ancient Dai Viet around the Red River delta became known to Europeans as Tongking, and the southern state as Cochin-China.

Cochin-China continued a policy of expansion. The Saigon area was under its control by 1690, and the remains of the Cambodia kingdom was under Vietnamese or Siamese overlordship for most of the 18th century. The Lao state of Lansang broke up in the

Annex
To incorporate a territory within another state.

17th century into three principalities that paid tribute to Siam, Tongking, or Cochin-China. The Tay-son rebellion of 1773–92 destroyed first Cochin-China and then Tongking, effectively reuniting the kingdom.

European and Islamic traders

After initially finding European guns and trade wealth useful, the major mainland states all began to fear European power. In 1688, an anti-foreigner revolution overthrew the Siamese monarchy, and both Siam and the Vietnamese states thereafter reoriented their trade toward the less threatening Chinese.

Spanish settlement of the Philippine Islands began in 1571 around Manila, which became the center for Spanish trade with Asia and for Christianizing the Philippines. The Islamic states of Sulu and Magindanao resisted Spanish control in the southern islands.

In the Indonesian archipelago, the sultanate of Malacca focused much of the trade between the Indian Ocean, China, and southeast Asia until 1511, when the Portuguese conquered the city and built a fort which they held until the Dutch took it in 1641. Muslim traders dispersed, strengthening the new Islamic powers of the 16th and 17th centuries, notably Aceh, Bantam, and Mataram. Farther east, the Portuguese built forts to control the supply of cloves and sandalwood but never overcame the Islamic trading network. By 1605, Macassar adopted Islam and became the main trade center of east Indonesia.

The Dutch East India Company (VOC) took control of Amboina in 1606, Jakarta in 1619, the Banda Islands in 1621, and monopolized clove production in the Moluccas. In the 18th century, its interest shifted to Java, including production of coffee and sugar, but its trade monopolies collapsed after 1770 in the face of stronger British, French, American, and Chinese trade.

Tribute
Payment by one state to another for protection or to indicate submission.

Curriculum Context

In world history curricula, students often analyze how and why Islam continued to expand in southeast Asia in the 16th and 17th centuries.

The Spanish–American Empire

Spain's exploration and conquest of the Americas brought wealth in the form of gold and silver, which became the basis of all European trade.

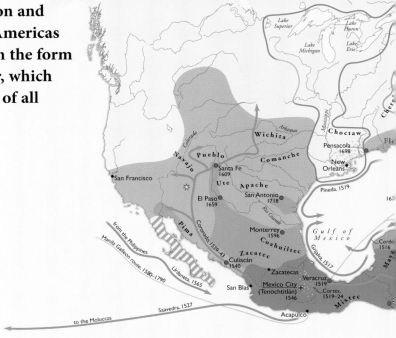

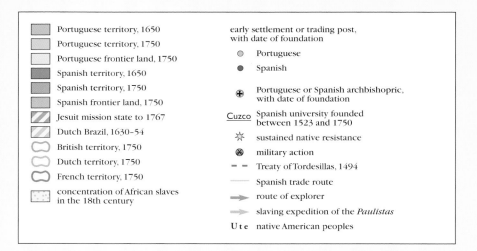

Portuguese territory, 1650	
Portuguese territory, 1750	
Portuguese frontier land, 1750	
Spanish territory, 1650	
Spanish territory, 1750	
Spanish frontier land, 1750	
Jesuit mission state to 1767	
Dutch Brazil, 1630–54	
British territory, 1750	
Dutch territory, 1750	
French territory, 1750	
concentration of African slaves in the 18th century	

early settlement or trading post, with date of foundation

◯   Portuguese

●   Spanish

✛   Portuguese or Spanish archbishopric, with date of foundation

Cuzco   Spanish university founded between 1523 and 1750

✵   sustained native resistance

✕   military action

– –   Treaty of Tordesillas, 1494

——   Spanish trade route

➤   route of explorer

➤   slaving expedition of the *Paulistas*

U t e   native American peoples

NORTH
ATLANTIC
OCEAN

Bermuda
Islands
to Britain

Columbus, 1492

Ponce de Leon, 1512–13

Havana–Cádiz direct route

Bahamas

1628

San Juan
1511

Puerto Rico

Lesser Antilles

Columbus, 1493

Island Arawak

Cuba

1511

Santo Domingo
1496

Hispaniola

Jamaica

Island Carib

Columbus, 1498

Ojeda & Vespucci, 1499

Magellan, 1519

Cabral, 1500

Armada Española route, to 1748

a Nueva España route 1580–1790

Columbus 1502–4

Cumaná
1521

Paramaribo

Cayenne

1640

Caracas
1567

Orinoco

Georgetown

Ceará

Natal
1597

Olinda
1537

Guahibo

Arawak

Carib

Guiana Highlands

Bele
do Pará
1616

São Luis
1615
Macantão

Recife
1563

1584,
1740
Cartagena
1533

Bastidas & La Cosa, 1501–2

MARANHÃO

Porto Bello
1597

Nombre de Dios
1510

1571

Panama
1519

1564

Santa Fe de Bogotá
1538

Chibcha

Macu

Timbira

1667

Bahia
1549

Pizarro 1526–27

Tierra Firme y Perú route, to 1746

1568, 1572,
1595, 1739

Witoto

Putumayo

Amazon

Manaus
1674

Madeira

Munducuru

Caraja

São Francisco

Santa
Cruz

to India

FIC
EAN

Quito
1534

Guayaquil
1535

Amazon
Basin

Cawahie

Ucayali

Brazilian
Highlands

Villa Rica
1698

Piro

Mato
Grosso
Plateau

Rio de Janeiro
1565

Mochica

ANDES

Pizarro 1533

Inca

Cuzco

La Paz

Nambicuara

São Paulo
1532

São Vicente
1530

Callao
1537

1546

Ciudad de
los Reyes
(Lima)
1535

Peru

Aymara

Nazca

1609

Chuquisaca
(Charcas/La Plata)
1538

Potosí
1545

Arica
1537

Asunción
1538

Guaraní

Paraná

Tupinamba

Buenos Aires–Cádiz route, from 1778

Portuguese
Spanish

to the Philippines

Araucanians

Córdoba
1573

Buenos
Aires
1536

Banda
Oriental

Magellan, 1519–20

SOUTH
ATLANTIC
OCEAN

Valparaiso
1541

Santiago
1541

ANDES

Spanish
Portuguese

Valdivia
1552

Patagonia

Magellan, 1520–21

The Spanish–American Empire

Spanish conquest in the New World profoundly affected both the region itself and Europe. It destroyed ancient cultures and decimated native populations. Meanwhile, the mining of huge silver deposits financed Spanish Habsburg ambitions and underpinned trade throughout Europe.

Spain's incursion in the Americas began with royal sponsorship of the voyages of the Italian navigator-merchants Christopher Columbus and Amerigo Vespucci at the end of the 15th century. Columbus' discovery of the West Indies for Spain soon led to permanent settlements. Colonization of the Caribbean islands began on Santo Domingo (Hispaniola) and provided a foretaste of Spanish rule on the mainland. Administrative, legal, and religious structures were rapidly put in place, while the aboriginal Arawak and Carib peoples fell victim to maltreatment and disease.

Aboriginal
Describes the earliest known people of a region.

Exploitation and conversion
The Spanish empire was concerned with the government, economic exploitation, and religious conversion of its native subjects. Its rapid growth depended on existing political structures and communications networks. Hernán Cortés and Francisco Pizarro encountered, in the Aztec and Inca empires respectively, centralized, populous, and formidable states, yet internal divisions helped them to destroy any resistance. Beyond their boundaries, the population was sparse and the environment hostile and virtually impenetrable to Europeans. These hinterlands were still only partially conquered by 1800.

Hinterlands
Remote regions.

Challenges to Spain
Challenges by Spain's European rivals to the Spanish–American empire were frequent but largely unsuccessful. From the 1570s, major ports were

subjected to numerous assaults. The British capture of Jamaica in 1655 was an important strategic loss, but the empire remained largely secure until the Seven Years' War (1756–63). In 1762, the British occupied Havana; Spain only regained control by ceding Florida. However, the demise of France as a colonial power in America allowed Spain to acquire Louisiana while, in the American Revolution, it regained Florida and checked British expansion on the Mississippi.

Gold and silver

The prosperity of Spain's empire was built above all on Mexican and Peruvian gold and silver. These precious metals had been extracted on a modest scale by the Aztecs and Incas for use in ceremonial artifacts, but were now mined and shipped in huge quantities by the Spanish. The enterprise required regular commercial fleets with permanent naval escorts, linking Seville and Veracruz on the east coast of Mexico, and Peru and the west coast of the Central American isthmus. The maintenance and protection of these fleets was one of the great maritime and commercial achievements of the age.

Brazil and the Portuguese

Portugal claimed the coast of Brazil, discovered by Pedro Alvares Cabral in 1500. From about 1530, the Portuguese began to settle Brazil in large numbers. Philip II's acquisiton of the Portuguese crown in 1580 drew the Portuguese colonies into the Dutch–Spanish War and, from the 1620s, Dutch efforts to capture Portugal's possessions provoked a limited but savage war. An alliance between the Portuguese and native Brazilians ultimately prevailed. Later, Portuguese slavers penetrated the Brazilian jungle to attack Spanish Jesuit missions on the fringes of Spanish possessions. In 1680, the Portuguese authorities banned the enslavement of native Americans and suppressed the slavers, but their expeditions had taken Portuguese control far into the continent's interior.

Curriculum Context

The role played by the Catholic church in colonial administration and in policies toward indigenous populations is an important aspect of the Spanish and Portuguese colonial empires.

Europeans in North America

European settlements were restricted to the coasts of North America, while explorers tried to find routes to the Pacific and Asia.

Bering, 1728

Cook, 1778

St Lawrence Island

Bering Sea

Cook, 1778

Inuit

Yukon

Inuit

Nunivak Island

Inuit

Ingalik

Aleutian Islands

Cook, 1778

Aleut

Kodiak Island

Chirikov, 1741

C O A S T

Tlingit

Arteaga & Quadra, 1779

Cook, 1778

Yukon

M O U N T

Gulf of Alaska

Chirikov, 1741

Queen Charlotte Island

Haida

Arteaga & Quadra, 1779

Vancouver Island

Cook, 1778

extent of European settlement by 1650

Dutch

English

French

Spanish

Swedish

☞ early European landing

European settlement or trading post founded in the 16th or 17th centuries

● Dutch

● English

● French

● Spanish

route of exploration (conjectural routes are shown dashed)

➡ England

➡ France

➡ Portugal

➡ Russia

➡ Spain

➡ raid by the Iroquois, 1642–89

Ute native American peoples

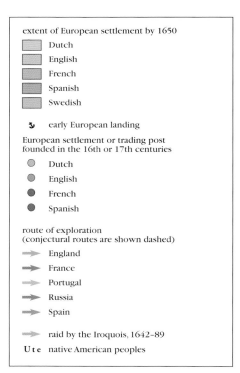

Europeans in North America

The exploration of North America was unlike other achievements of the age of European expansion. Even though many of the cultures and civilizations encountered in other continents had had little recent contact with Europeans, they were not all wholly alien.

Until the 18th century, North America remained enigmatic. Its true scale was not appreciated, nor did it offer any immediate returns on the investments of explorers and their backers.

Passage to Asia

The earliest explorers chanced upon North America while seeking a route to China; Columbus died convinced that he had found an island off the Asian mainland. After Giovanni da Verrazano had explored the length of the Atlantic seaboard and the first colonial ventures had encountered a densely wooded interior and native peoples hostile to exploration inland, the search began for a route around the continent. A possible northern passage remained an English obsession: Hudson, Davis, and Baffin endured hardships in the Canadian north to find a northwest sea passage to China. Even James Cook, mapping the Alaskan coast in 1778–79, felt compelled to explore major inlets in search of the elusive seaway.

Curriculum Context

Students can use historical maps to trace routes taken by early explorers from the 15th through the 17th century around Africa, to the Americas, and across the Pacific.

River exploration

French exploration of the St. Lawrence River was stimulated by the idea of a sea passage through the heart of the continent. Cartier, Champlain, the Jesuit fathers, the de la Vérendryes, and generations of fur trappers progressed down the St. Lawrence and through the Great Lakes, fueling the myth of a route westward. This myth finally evaporated in the Great Plains beyond Lake Manitoba. La Salle's descent of the Mississippi in 1682 revealed a north–south passage, yet his disappointment at finding the Gulf of Mexico rather than the Pacific was profound.

Exploring the continent

Initial Spanish exploration of North America from Mexico and the Caribbean under leaders such as de Soto and Coronado was mounted in a spirit of conquest, gold-lust, and missionary zeal. Large military expeditions were equipped to build forts, establish missions, and despoil the cities that reputedly lay to the north. After epic journeys, survivors of these expeditions returned exhausted and empty-handed. By the early 17th century, Spanish New Mexico was little more than a string of outposts in the pueblo villages around Santa Fé, surrounded by desert. Florida, which the Spaniards initially believed to be an island, was explored for strategic reasons to protect the Spanish bullion fleet route to Europe. Similarly, the Spaniards ventured up the Californian coast in the 17th century in response to a combined British and Russian threat.

Moving westward

By the 1650s, only the European colonies of the Atlantic seaboard had attracted settlers in number, and it was here that the true wealth of the American continent—rich farmland—began to be exploited. From the outset, the Dutch New Netherland colony encouraged settlement by farmers, while the English colonies quickly developed a European-style agricultural economy. The native peoples welcomed settlers for the trade they brought but they prevented expansion inland. The Appalachian mountains also remained a formidable barrier. It was 180 years after Cabot's landing before English traders and explorers penetrated the basin of the Ohio, after European diseases and the erosion of native cultures had weakened resistance. In the years following the British conquest of French America, the trickle of pioneers across the Appalachians and into the fertile lands of Kentucky and Tennessee became a flood, marking a new era of truly profitable exploration.

Mission

A base for Catholic priests who came as missionaries to spread Christianity among the Native Americans, also used as a colonial administrative center.

Curriculum Context

Not all European nations had the same motives for exploration in North America. It might be revealing to compare English, French, Spanish, and Dutch motives.

Basin

The area of land drained by a river and its tributaries.

Colonial North America

From 1650, conflicts between
France, Britain, and the
Netherlands spread to North
America and involved its Native
American population.

extent of European settlement in 1713

- British
- French
- Spanish

French territory acquired by Britain, 1713

European territorial claims, 1750

- British
- French
- Spanish

British territory after 1763

Spanish territory after 1763

settlement or trading post founded
in the 18th century

- British
- French
- Spanish

French and Indian War, 1755–63

- British capture of fort or settlement
- French capture of fort or settlement
- British victory
- French victory
- Spanish victory
- raid by French and native allies on British settlements
- British campaign
- Spanish campaign
- Iroquois campaign, 1642–67
- migration of Delaware and Shawnee, 1730–55
- colonial road
- trade route of the native peoples

Ute   native American peoples

Southampton Island

Coats Island

Mansel Island

Labrador Sea

Inuit

Inuit

Hudson Bay

Naskapi

Belcher Islands

Newfoundland

Newfoundland

St John's

Fort York

Fort Severn

Rupert's Land (Hudson's Bay Company)

Akimiski Island

Eastern Cree

⊗ 1746

Louisbourg 1758

Ile St Jean (Prince Edward I)

Ile Royale (Cape Breton I)

Fort Albany

Moose Factory

Fort Rupert

Tadoussac

Ft Beauséjour 1755

Montagnais

Nova Scotia

Halifax

Cree

Fort La Tourette

Ojibwa

Plains of Abraham 1759

⊗ 1711

Québec 1759

Port Royal 1710

Fort Népigon

Trois Rivières

Montréal 1760

New France

St Lawrence

Fort Maurepas

Fort St Pierre

Fort Michipicten

Huron

Lake Superior

Crown Point 1759

Ticonderoga 1758

New Hampshire

Portsmouth

Fort Kaministiquia

Sault St Marie

Fort William Henry 1756

Fort Frontenac 1758

Fort George 1756

1704

Boston

Massachusetts

St es

Lake Huron

Fort Rouillé

Fort Oswego 1756

Fort Ontario 1755

Albany

Plymouth

Providence

Gros entre

Fort St Croix

Winnebago

Fort Niagara

Lake Michigan

Lake Ontario

New York

New Haven

Connecticut

ndan

Ottawa

Pennsylvania

New Amsterdam until 1664

New Jersey

oux

Fort Beauharnais

Fort St Joseph

Lake Erie

Fort Presqu'isle

Philadelphia

Delaware

Mississippi

Miami Wyandot

Fort Pontchartrain

Fort Duquesne 1758

Fort Necessity 1755

Delaware

Baltimore

Annapolis

Maryland

ATLANTIC OCEAN

Fort St Louis

Fort Crevecoeur

Fort Pickawillany 1752

Shawnee

Ohio

Virginia

Richmond

Williamsburg

Jamestown

Kaintuck

Warrior's Path

Fort Vincennes

Fort Orléans

Tuscarora

North Carolina

New Bern

Fort Chartres

APPALACHIAN MTS

Decaneechi Path

Wilmington

Louisiana

Great Trading Path

Cherokee

South Carolina

Georgetown

Chickasaw

Fort Prudhomme

Fort Augusta

Charleston

Choctaw

Creek

1742 ⊗ Savannah

Georgia

Alabama

Fort King George

Yamassee

1740, 1743

St Augustine 1702

Fort Rosalie

Fort Condé

Pensacola

Natchez

New Orleans

Florida

Gulf of Mexico

Colonial North America

From the 1650s, most major European wars were also fought out in North America. The Dutch took New Sweden (Delaware) from Louis XIV's European ally in 1655. Likewise, the New Netherland colony (in the Hudson River region) was overrun by English forces during the Anglo–Dutch naval wars (1664).

The main rivalry was between the French and the British. Early exploration had created distinct areas of influence on the St. Lawrence and the eastern seaboard respectively. As these grew to include claims in the Mississippi basin, Georgia, and the Appalachian foothills, some native peoples were drawn into the hostility between the colonists.

Curriculum Context

In some states, students are asked to understand the significance of colonial wars before 1754.

Early Anglo–French conflicts

Sporadic fighting erupted when a French expedition sacked English trading forts on Hudson Bay (1686) and French and Huron raids ravaged New England, despite England's alliance with the Iroquois. Britain seized the opportunity of Queen Anne's War (the War of the Spanish Succession) to overrun the French territory of Acadia in 1710. Renamed Nova Scotia, the peninsula was confirmed as a British possession (together with Newfoundland) by the Treaty of Utrecht in 1713, while the Ile St. Jean and Ile Royale remained French. However, the area remained the scene of regular skirmishes for 50 years. In King George's War—the War of the Austrian Succession—the French naval base at Louisbourg on Ile Royale was sacked (1745), a French naval expedition to reconquer Acadia was destroyed by a storm (1746), and an unsuccessful British and Iroquois attack on New France led to widespread French and Huron raids (1746–48). Hostilities continued after the war in the Ohio basin, where the French tried to halt British expansion westward by destroying the advanced post at Pickawillany.

Skirmish

A minor battle.

The French and Indian War

The decisive phase of Anglo-French conflict came with the French and Indian War (1755–63). The European population of New France and Louisiana was only one-tenth that of the British colonies; despite strategically sited forts and alliances with the indigenous peoples, the French could no longer offset this imbalance. The British navy blockaded both trade and military reinforcements from France. Initially, Britain suffered defeat at Fort Duquesne, failed to take Crown Point, and endured successful French counterattacks and defeat at Ticonderoga (1758). Thereafter, the war swung in Britain's favor. Wolfe's victory near Québec in 1759 secured British supremacy. By 1760, the whole of New France was in British hands. At the same time, British naval forces captured all French possessions in the West Indies except Saint-Domingue. When France coerced Spain to enter the war, the British occupied Florida and Havana. In the Treaty of Paris (1763), Britain's control of the whole of North America east of the Mississippi was confirmed. French territories beyond the Mississippi passed to Spain, which also regained Havana in exchange for Florida.

Curriculum Context

An important aspect of the French and Indian War for Britain, France, and Spain was its effect on the indigenous peoples in their colonial territories.

The impact on Native Americans

Contact with Europeans initially brought some benefits to indigenous peoples: in the southwest, the Plains peoples reverted to buffalo-hunting after acquiring Spanish horses; in the mid 17th century, the Huron people of the Great Lakes were saved by their military alliance with France from destruction by the Iroquois. However, native Americans experienced a steady loss of their traditional lands. King Philip's War of 1675–76 ended native resistance to European encroachment in the northeast; the Tuscarora and Yamassee peoples were driven out of the Carolinas in 1711 and 1715 respectively; and from 1730 to 1755, the Shawnee and Delaware fled west down the Ohio. Only in the west was European impact minimal.

Curriculum Context

The relationships between Native Americans and Spanish, English, French, and Dutch settlers were complex and highly influential in the course of later American history.

The American Revolution

Britain had won the struggle with France for domination of North America, but the diverse European settlers increasingly resented British interference.

Lake Winnipeg

Fort Népigon

Fort William

Winnipeg

Fort St Charles

Mississippi

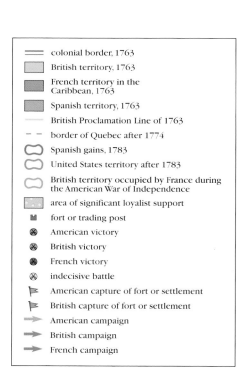

───	colonial border, 1763
▢	British territory, 1763
▢	French territory in the Caribbean, 1763
▢	Spanish territory, 1763
───	British Proclamation Line of 1763
─ ─	border of Quebec after 1774
⬭	Spanish gains, 1783
⬭	United States territory after 1783
⬭	British territory occupied by France during the American War of Independence
▢	area of significant loyalist support
⛫	fort or trading post
⊗	American victory
⊗	British victory
⊗	French victory
⊗	indecisive battle
⚑	American capture of fort or settlement
⚑	British capture of fort or settlement
➜	American campaign
➜	British campaign
➜	French campaign

Albany •Fort Rupert
Factory

Rupert's Land
(Hudson's Bay Company)

Québec

Canada

Harricana

St Lawrence

Montréal
1775

Montgomery, 1775

Fort
Ticonderoga
1775

Arnold, 1775

Falmouth

Burgoyne, 1777

Lake
Ontario

Fort Oswego

Fort
Stanwix

Saratoga
1777

Albany

Oriskany
1777

St Leger, 1777

Fort Niagara

Lake
Huron

Lake
Erie

Fort
Pontchartrain

Fort Sandusky

Fort Pitt

New York

New Hampshire

Massachusetts

Lexington
1775

Bunker Hill
1775
Boston
1776

Massachusetts

Providence

Newport

Rhode Island
Connecticut

Rochambeau,
1780

New Haven

Rochambeau, 1780

White Plains
1776

Long Island
1776

New Jersey

Pennsylvania

Princeton
1777

Trenton
1776

Valley Forge

Philadelphia
1777

Brandywine
1777

William Howe, 1777

de Barras, 1781

Delaware

Baltimore

Maryland

La Fayette
1781

1781

Washington
1781

Clark, 1778

Ohio

Boonesborough

Harrodsburg

Native American Territory

Tennessee

Yorktown
1781

Richmond

Petersburg

Virginia

Roanoke

Chesapeake Capes
1781

de Grasse, 1781

Cornwallis, 1781

Guilford Court
House
1781

Cornwallis, 1781

North Carolina

Wilmington

King's Mountain
1780

Cowpens
1781

Camden
1780

Eutaw Springs
1781

South Carolina

Augusta

Charleston
1780

Clinton & Cornwallis 1780

Campbell, 1778

Georgia

Savannah
1778

Prevost, 1778

St Augustine

East Florida

West Florida

Pensacola

New Orleans

Chestahoochee

Alabama

Altamaha

ATLANTIC
OCEAN

Halifax

Nova
Scotia

William Howe, 1776

Lord Howe, 1776

William Howe, 1776

Quebec

Appalachian Mts

Inset (Caribbean):

Puerto Rico

Anguilla

St Eustace
St Kitts   Barbuda
1782
Nevis   Antigua
Montserrat

Leeward Islands

Guadeloupe

Marie-Galante

The Saintes
1782
Dominica

1780
Martinique

Windward Islands
1781
St Lucia

St Vincent

Caribbean
Sea

Barbados

1779   Grenada

Trinidad   Tobago

0   200 km
0   300 mi

The American Revolution

The 18th century witnessed a great increase in the colonial population of North America, particularly with the end of the struggle for supremacy between Britain and France in 1763. In just five years between 1769 and 1774, 152 ships from Irish ports alone brought over 44,000 new colonists.

Curriculum Context

In some states, students are expected to be able to assess the moral, political, and cultural influence of Protestant Christianity on the Thirteen Colonies.

Loyalist

Supporting the government or the sovereign.

By 1774, Europeans in North America numbered two million. This growth altered the nature of the colonies and the allegiances of their inhabitants.

Germans, Irish, and Scots

In Pennsylvania, a flood of German and Irish Protestant immigrants in the 1720s outnumbered the original English Quakers. German soldiers sent to the colonies by the Hanoverian dynasty ruling Britain further swelled the non-British populace; Scots and Irish settlers, many with Jacobite (anti-Hanoverian) sympathies, also arrived.

After 1775, loyalist support was concentrated in those longer-established colonies whose inhabitants could claim English ancestry. Even so, Virginia and the Carolinas, which attracted few non-British immigrants and were developing a distinctive plantation economy based on mass importation of slaves, showed little enthusiasm for the loyalist cause.

Trade Restrictions

The influx of new immigrants, together with a rising birthrate in the colonies, are evidence of a booming economy. Agriculture was by far the most important activity, but it was commerce (particularly that of New England) that caused Britain most concern. Mercantilist theory maintained that colonial possessions should be developed to supply goods or raw materials unavailable in the home country, that these commodities should be paid for in manufactured goods for the colonists, and that the colonies should be discouraged from engaging in any other form of external trade. From the mid-17th century onward, these theories were imposed on the British colonies through a range of legislation, including the 1651 and 1673 Trade and Navigation Acts and the 1663 Staple Act. Yet the introduction of European-style agriculture into North America compromised the first of these conditions, while application of the second caused a currency shortage that rendered useless any attempts to restrict independent colonial trade.

Curriculum Context

Understanding the social, economic, and political tensions that existed will explain the conflicts between the colonists and their governments.

Smuggling

By the 18th century, the economy relied on smuggling: that is, trade other than with Britain. Merchants traded in fish, whale oil, horses, beef, and timber to the Spanish, Dutch, and French Caribbean in exchange for sugar, molasses, rum, and silver coin. By the 1750s, they had begun to export dried fish, grain, and flour to Europe in their own vessels, competing with British shippers and often bypassing British ports. In response, customs administration was tightened, and a succession of laws passed in Britain from 1763 sought to curb this trade, including the 1764 Sugar Act. Along with the imposition of direct taxation in the Stamp Act of 1763, these caused great resentment in America.

New Taxes

At the same time, the costs that had been incurred in the war to gain control of the French colonies proved a severe drain on Britain's finances. In 1763–65, prime minister George Grenville forced the colonies to bear a greater share of this cost by imposing a series of taxes and other obligations. All colonial goods carried on British ships were subject to duty, for example, even if they were not headed for Britain. One provision that caused particular resentment was the Quartering Act of 1765, providing for the quartering of soldiers in colonial public buildings; it was seen as irrelevant once the French threat had dissipated.

Prime minister

The head of the British government.

Curriculum Context

Reconstructing the chronology of the events leading to armed conflict between the American colonies and England is included in many curricula.

Colonial Expansion Restricted

Finally, the British attempted to forestall further hostilities over land with the indigenous peoples by setting limits to colonial expansion. The 1763 Proclamation Line defined a theoretical western boundary to the growth of the colonies. This aroused opposition (and was largely disregarded) in America, where the open frontier had already become an essential element in economic growth and the absorption of new immigrants. The 1774 Quebec Act, which provided for the government of former French colonies and extended Quebec's boundaries to the Ohio and Mississippi, was widely seen as a further attempt to restrict colonial freedom.

War with Britain

These issues combined to produce escalating tension between the colonists and their British governors. Among the colonists momentum developed for change, fanned by the activities of correspondence committees, which used the mail service to exchange complaints about the British and suggestions for change. The colonists formed militias of Minutemen to protect themselves, rather than rely on British troops. When militias clashed with the British at Lexington and Concord near Boston in 1775, the exchanges of fire heralded the coming of open war. Despite early reverses against the Patriot army, commanded by George Washington, the British commanders Sir William Howe and his brother Admiral Lord Howe had regained the initiative by the second year of the war, by capitalizing on the strategic mobility that their naval supremacy afforded. Meanwhile, representatives of the Thirteen Colonies had gathered to discuss developments at a Continental Congress at Philadelphia. The momentous outcome was the Declaration of Independence. Drafted largely by Thomas Jefferson, the Declaration was in large part a list of colonial grievances against the British—and in

Curriculum Context

By reconstructing the arguments among patriots and loyalists about independence, conclusions can be drawn about how the decision to declare independence was reached.

part a revolutionary statement of the god-given rights of the Americans to govern themselves.

On the battlefield, subsequent campaigns confirmed to the British the difficulty of holding large territories against an increasingly hostile population. The British suffered a number of defeats before the Battle of Saratoga in October 1777, when the loss of a major British army marked the end of any prospect of an invasion from British Canada.

Victory at Saratoga was a turning point in the conflict. It not only encouraged the Patriots, who had previously been somewhat demoralized—but also alerted foreign powers to the possibility of an ultimate American victory. That drew increased support from both France and Spain—but it was the intervention of France that ultimately proved decisive. The victory of a French fleet over the Royal Navy off the Chesapeake Capes forced the surrender of a besieged British army at Yorktown in 1781. Although Britain saved the economically vital West Indies by defeating a French invasion fleet in the eastern Caribbean in 1782, the American colonies were lost irretrievably. The Treaty of Paris of 1783 confirmed the independence of the new United States of America.

Curriculum Context

An explanation of how the Americans won the war against superior British resources is required in many curricula.

Besieged

Surrounded by armed forces.

Curriculum Context

It is important to analyze the terms of the Treaty of Paris to understand how they affected U.S. relations with Native Americans and with European powers in North America.

Glossary

Aboriginal Describes the earliest known people of a region.

Ancien régime A term for the old political and social systems prevalent in Europe up to the end of the 18th century, in which monarchs, clergy, and aristocrats were dominant.

Annex To incorporate a territory within another state.

Artillery The section of an army that uses heavy weaponry, such as cannons and rockets.

Bankruptcy The legal state of being financially ruined.

Basin The area of land drained by a river and its tributaries.

Besieged Surrounded by armed forces.

Blockade To deploy ships or troops to prevent supplies or reinforcements reaching an enemy state.

Boyar A Russian high noble, ranked below a ruling prince.

Bullion Bars or ingots of gold or silver.

Bureaucracy A government with fixed rules, specialized functions, and a clear hierarchy of authority.

Capitalism An economic system that includes private investment of money, and prices and production of goods determined by competition in a free market.

Caste A social class with its own occupations and restrictions.

Clan A group of people with a common ancestor.

Client state A state that is dependent on another country economically, militarily, or politically.

Corsair Describes pirates, usually off the north African coast.

Diocese The territory under the authority of a bishop.

Edict A proclamation of a law.

Elector One of the German princes entitled to take part in choosing the Holy Roman emperor.

Fealty The loyalty of a vassal or tenant to his lord.

Hegemony Influence or authority over others.

Hinterlands Remote regions.

Huguenot French Protestant

Imam A Muslim spiritual and political leader.

Jesuit Order The Society of Jesus, a Roman Catholic order founded by Saint Ignatius Loyola in 1534 to carry out missionary and educational work, and attempt to halt the spread of Protestantism.

Khanate A state composed of Turkish, Tatar, or Mongol tribes, ruled by a khan.

Loyalist Supporting the government or the sovereign.

Mercenary Hired foreign soldier.

Mission A base for Catholic priests who came as missionaries to spread Christianity among the Native Americans, also used as a colonial administrative center.

Naval stores The raw materials needed for shipbuilding, such as timber, flax, hemp, pitch, and tar.

Oligarchy A government controlled by a small group of people.

Planted Deliberately sent to colonize an area for political reasons.

Prime minister The head of the British government.

Protégé Someone who is protected and trained.

Proxy war A war fought over a country that itself does not take part in the war.

Regent Someone who governs a state when the sovereign is absent, or too young or disabled to rule.

Revocation The taking back, or revoking, of a law.

Sack To capture and plunder.

Scorched-earth tactics The deliberate destruction of property and resources, so that an invading army cannot use them.

Serfdom The state of being a serf, having to work on the land and be subject to the will of the land's owner.

Skirmish A minor battle.

Steppe A vast area of grassland stretching across eastern Europe and Asia.

Sultanate A Muslim state governed by a sultan.

Tribute Payment by one state to another for protection or to indicate submission.

Vassal status Having to obey another state in return for protection.

Vizier A high-ranking executive officer in a Muslim state.

Further Research

BOOKS

Anderson, Fred. *Crucible of War: The Seven Years' War and the Fate of Empire in British North America, 1754–1766*. Vintage, 2001.

Anderson, Fred. *The War That Made America: A Short History of the French and Indian War*. Penguin, 2006.

Blanning, Tim. *The Pursuit of Glory: the Five Revolutions that Made Modern Europe: 1648–1815*. Penguin, 2008.

Crossley, Pamela Kyle. *The Manchus*. Wiley-Blackwell, 2002.

Dunn, Richard S. *The Age of Religious Wars, 1559–1715*. W. W. Norton & Company, 1979.

Eckert, Allan W. *Wilderness America: A Narrative*. Jesse Stuart Foundation, 2001.

Ehret, Christopher. *The Civilizations of Africa: A History to 1800*. University of Virginia Press, 2002.

Elliott, J. H. *Empires of the Atlantic World: Britain and Spain in America, 1492–1830*. Yale University Press, 2007.

Elliott, J. H. *Europe Divided: 1559–1598*. Wiley-Blackwell, 2000.

Elliott, J. H. *Imperial Spain: 1469–1716*. Penguin, 2002.

Eraly, Abraham. *The Mughal Throne: The Saga of India's Great Emperors*. Phoenix, 2004.

Hanks, Merry E. Wiesner. *Early Modern Europe, 1450–1789*. Cambridge University Press, 2006.

Ingrao, Charles W. *The Habsburg Monarchy, 1618–1815*. Cambridge University Press, 2000.

Kort, Michael. *A Brief History of Russia*. Checkmark Books, 2008.

MacCulloch, Diarmaid. *The Reformation*. Penguin, 2005.

Middlekauff, Robert. *The Glorious Cause: The American Revolution, 1763–1789*. Oxford University Press, USA, 2007.

Parker, Geoffrey. *Europe in Crisis: 1598–1648*. Wiley-Blackwell, 2001.

Tarling, Nicholas, ed. *The Cambridge History of Southeast Asia (Part 2)*. Cambridge University Press, 2000.

Taylor, Alan. *American Colonies: The Settling of North America.* Penguin, 2002.

Totman, Conrad. *A History of Japan.* Wiley-Blackwell, 2005.

Wedgwood, C. V. *The Thirty Years' War.* NYRB Classics, 2005.

INTERNET RESOURCES

American Revolution.com. Contains a history, historical documents, people, and resources.
www.americanrevolution.com

History of China. Includes articles on all the dynasties with maps and illustrations.
www.history-of-china.com

International World History Project. A collection of essays, documents, and maps on world history.
www.history-world.org

Internet Modern History Sourcebook. Contains thousands of sources for European and American history in the early modern world.
www.fordham.edu/halsall/modsbook.html

Iran Chamber Society. Includes a section on the Safavid empire 1502–1736.
www.iranchamber.com/history/safavids.php

Louis XIV – the Sun King. Includes biography, politics, religion, and wars.
www.louis-xiv.de

Macrohistory and World Report. This site includes useful information in the section 16th to 19th centuries.
www.fsmitha.com

TheOttomans.org. A detailed history of the Ottomans, century by century.
www.theottomans.org/english/history/index.asp

The Reformation. The story of the struggle between the Catholic Church and Protestantism in Europe.
www.thereformation.info

The Story of Africa: African History from the Dawn of Time. A comprehensive history of the continent.
www.bbc.co.uk/worldservice/specials/1624_story_of_africa/index.shtml

Index